A History of Greenwich

A History

Aerial view of archaeological excavations at Greenwich in 1971

# of Greenwich

Beryl Platts

Second Edition

PROCTER PRESS · LONDON

By the same author
ORIGINS OF HERALDRY
SCOTTISH HAZARD

Set in 11/13pt Plantin

ISBN 0 906650 02 X

First published in 1973 by
David and Charles Ltd
Newton Abbot, Devon

This edition
THE PROCTER PRESS
Greenwich
London S.E.10
1986

Printed and bound in Great Britain by
Biddles Ltd, Guildford and King's Lynn

To Elizabeth and John
whose loving forbearance
has made the writing of this book
such a pleasure

Contents

List of Illustrations

Preface to the 1986 Edition

When I first embarked on a history of Greenwich, I saw my task as twofold. For many years there had been an overwhelming academic need to collate all that was known about the town, from official documents and old accounts, and to set it into a coherent framework of history, both local and national. This, within the scope of a short book, I have tried to do. It was also apparent that Edward Hasted's description of the Greenwich of Henry V as no more than a small fishing town was seriously misleading. The Rev. Thomas Streatfeild and his colleagues followed and repeated this teaching when they decided to amplify Hasted's account of the Hundred of Blackheath, even though much of the huge weight of material they collected was in direct opposition to such a description. The consequent dismissal of Greenwich from modern reference books as a place of any earlier importance resulted in a gap in our national historical knowledge, amounting in some aspects almost to a distortion. This gap I have attempted to bridge, knowing that more historical and archaeological investigation would be necessary before it could be entirely filled.

But the greatest need for a history of Greenwich lay in its vulnerability without one. Much of the vandalism, both public and private, which characterised the postwar years and has torn the heart out of towns and villages all over England arose, as it seemed to me, out of ignorance. Greenwich was not without its champions, but those people wishing to bring evidence forward for the preservation of historic sites here, lacked a printed source to quote.

Researching into Greenwich history has all but persuaded me that it is inexhaustible; and I must apologise to those enthusiasts whose favourite section of it has seemed to be neglected. The building of what is now the Royal Naval College has been left out because it is dealt with elsewhere, as has the history of the Royal Observatory. Eltham deserves a story of its own; so do the dockyards of Deptford and Woolwich. What began as an account of a Hundred has inevitably, with the increasing complications of modernity, narrowed into the history of a parish. Not without regret for the lost chapters, I have seen my job as the setting up of a framework, for future historians to expand as they wish.

Almost all histories of England and biographies of English monarchs contain information specifically about Greenwich, not always recognised as such. Where I have quoted from those sources I have indicated them in the text. It would be impractical to catalogue general works of that kind for all the small references, however important some of them might later turn out to be, and I can only suggest to the student of Greenwich history that he should keep his eyes ever open for hidden local facts. By far the richest quarry for documentary reference is the *Hundred of Blackheath*, started by Streatfeild in 1829; a huge, confused pile of paper which overwhelmed four men before it was edited into some kind of order by H. H. Drake in 1886. A more readable source of local history is that printed in the *Transactions* of the Greenwich and Lewisham Antiquarian Society; and it is with great pleasure that I record here the profit I have gained from being associated with that body.

There is a wealth of material, much of it unpublished, in the Greenwich Local History Library. The Lewisham Local History Library has useful material about the manor of Old

Court and its environs. Many of the prehistoric and Romano-British objects found in the Greenwich district are cared for at the Plumstead Museum. But in a local history of this kind, it is often private papers that can provide the sudden illuminating gleam, and all those friends who have allowed me to look at documents concerning their houses have added truth and weight to this book.

Some sections of it first appeared in *Country Life*, and I am grateful to the then editor, Mr J. K. Adams, for permission to re-use them here. I am also personally in the debt of my colleagues on that magazine, whose unrivalled knowledge in the field of architectural history has been freely available to me, and two of whom, Arthur Oswald and Christopher Hussey, taught me how to research.

Many records of Greenwich are visual, and much may be gleaned from a study of old drawings and paintings of a place whose dramatic geography does not change. So the kindness of all those people, professional academics or scholarly amateurs, who have drawn my attention to small, significant points in such pictures – or indeed to pictures themselves, hanging obscurely on private walls – must not be under-estimated. I am grateful to Mr David Green for making available to me the photograph of Le Nôtre's plan for Greenwich Park, and to Viscount De L'Isle for the Penshurst picture, *Queen Elizabeth Dancing with Robert Dudley, Earl of Leicester*. The Ministry of Defence (Royal Navy) and the Captain of the Royal Naval College, Greenwich, kindly allowed me to reproduce a photograph of the archaeological excavations under the Admiral's lawn there; and I must express my particular thanks to its director, Dr Philip Dixon, for information imparted during the course of the dig. An exciting new dig was undertaken in 1978–79, at the Roman villa site in Greenwich Park under the direction of Mr Harvey Sheldon. Official reports on both these archaeological excavations are expected soon; they will add much to our history.

In the decade and a half since this book was first published, a good deal has changed in Greenwich – yet more has remained the same. The fearsome plans for a motorway across the park, culminating in a 19-lane intersection on the steps of St Alfege's, were quashed in response to a national outcry; but the devastation caused by the local authority in Stockwell and Burney streets remains, a shocking wound at the heart of the town. Some insensitive schemes of modern planners have been thwarted, others have merely shifted their focus; and the need for vigilance on the part of the people who live here is as constant as it was in the unhappy sixties.

In some ways Greenwich is a more prosperous place than it was in 1972. Because their history is now known and valued, most of the old properties are well looked after. The shopping streets have lost that air of despair and decay which characterised the post-way years, and fewer traders now go bankrupt. The street markets have brought a vitality into the town which, along with its atmosphere of pavement participation, creates an enjoyment that at times seems almost medieval. Traffic increases, but so do the crowds of appreciative visitors. And because more history is known, and set properly in its context, they get – and give – more profit from their visits.

In the end, however, a region's quality lies less with its tourists than its residents. The responsibility for Greenwich rests, as it always has, with its own people. To all the many inhabitants, past and present, who have valued this beautiful place and sought to preserve its identity, our debt is incalculable.

BERYL PLATTS
Greenwich, 1986

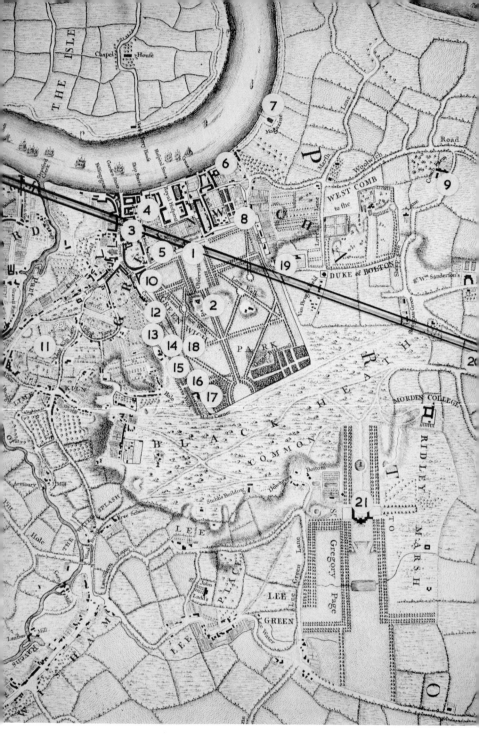

Map of Greenwich

Key

The map opposite shows a view of Greenwich, from the Survey of London made by John Rocque in 1746. Superimposed on it is the line of the Roman road discussed in Chapter 1. Other historic sites are indicated by numbers:

1 Tudor gatehouse, later Queen's House
2 Greenwich Tower or Castle, later Observatory
3 Swanne House
4 Leicester, later Arundel House
5 Copped Hall
6 Cogan House, later Crowley House
7 Enderby's Wharf
8 Sir Gregory Page's first house, later Vansittarts'
9 Combe Farm
10 Town well
11 The Ditches
12 Osboldston, later Cottle, later Olivier House
13 Dr Mason's house
14 Sir William Hooker's waste villas
15 First Snape villa, once the Wolfes' home, now Macartney House
16 Second Snape villa, Lord Chesterfield's Babiole, later owned by the Hulses
17 Third Snape villa, Montague House, pulled down by the Prince Regent in 1815
18 Burial ground
19 Vanbrugh's Castle
20 The forking Roman roads, noted by Dr Plot in 1690. The south fork would lead to Deptford Bridge
21 Wricklemarsh

CHAPTER 1

Roman Greenwich and its Predecessor

In the first week of February 1902 a discovery of profound importance was made at Greenwich. 'It came about,' wrote A. D. Webster, park superintendent, in his book, *Greenwich Park, its History and Associations*, 'in a simple way. When trying to locate the position of several barrows, and the site of Watling Street, the mound on which the remains have been found was, along with several others, mapped out as likely to afford traces which would be a guide to further observation.' On 6 February, while the park staff were working near by, 'a search was made in the mound by probing the soil with an iron bar. As a result several tesserae and cement were discovered, which at once confirmed the existence of Roman remains.'

The surprise was that such a find had not been made before. Over the years a number of objects, traces of a Roman presence in Greenwich, had been unearthed in the vicinity of the palace and the park. Burial urns were dug up in the garden of Dartmouth House, on Blackheath, in 1803; various remains suggestive of domestic structures had been uncovered during the building of the Victorian and Edwardian villas of Westcombe Park Road, outside the park on its eastern side; on the flat ground between the park hills and the river several highly significant finds had been made—a tessellated pavement near the power station; something that A. D. Webster described as 'a Roman medal'; a stone coffin; a gold piece of the first century, found near the

Admiral's lawn at the Royal Naval College; a bronze lamp dredged up from the Thames; and, perhaps the most telling find of all, a fasces—the symbolic axe bound round with rods which was carried by the lictors who preceded the chief magistrate of a city. Archaeology has only lately become an exact science, and, unfortunately, all too often the name of the finder, the precise location of the find and its ultimate destination were left unrecorded.

But there was nothing unrecordable about the building which now began to emerge from the southernmost of the mounds at the back of One Tree Hill, in Greenwich Park. The excavations were in charge of Mr Webster, as park superintendent, and Herbert Jones, a local antiquarian who had had valuable experience with professional archaeologists in the West Country. North Kent is a district short of natural building material, and far too much of these remains had been removed by the stone robbers for a coherent structure to be mapped out; but it was possible to see that this had been a substantial edifice of considerable importance, with tiled roof, tessellated floors, and outer walls not less than 2ft thick. Inner decoration had been elegant, perhaps even sumptuous; as many as twelve different patterns of painted plaster were found, and some green porphyry, finely polished on one side. 'If this has been part of a wall lining,' commented Herbert Jones, the excavator, 'the chamber it belonged to must have been highly decorated and of great beauty.'

But what function the building served could not be determined. All the clues pointed to the fact that it had been inhabited for a long time—perhaps throughout the whole four hundred years of Roman occupation. Three pieces of Bath stone, apparently sections of small columns about 8in in diameter, seemed to indicate that it had an outer corridor or verandah under the main roof, from which access could be gained to the different rooms. Objects found in the debris included many fragments of pottery, much of it, understandably, from the kilns at Upchurch on the Medway;

some four hundred coins extending in date from the Claudian invasion of AD 43 to the reign of Honorius (395–423); a draped arm from a well-made female statue; several fragments of inscriptions, some marble, some sandstone, but unfortunately all unreadable; and an assortment of bronze, ivory, iron and glass fragments, the latter including pieces of window glass.

It was not so much the discovery of this building, exciting though that was, as the implications of a Roman settlement at Greenwich that brought Roman scholars of the early twentieth century to their toes. Professor Francis Haverfield himself, it was murmured, on being told that a Roman villa had been uncovered in Greenwich Park, threw a handful of *denarii* out of his office window into the courtyard of the British Museum and cried: 'Come quickly! At last we have found Noviomagus!'

Evidence for the existence of the lost city of Noviomagus is present in the *Antonine Itinerary*, that ancient road book giving all the stations in the Roman Empire, produced probably as a result of surveys made during the reign of Augustus Caesar, apparently revised in the third century AD, and preserved in manuscript form through many copies until it was printed in Paris in 1512. Various English scholars then produced versions dealing with the English part. Even as late as the sixteenth century it was obvious from Roman remains still extant that the *Itinerary* was substantially correct, such small errors as were discoverable being due less to the inaccuracy of Roman surveyors than to mistakes and mis-readings in a thousand years of copying hands.

Not surprisingly, the name Noviomagus—which can best be translated as 'Newtown'—occurs a number of times throughout the *Itinerary*. The very slender contemporary documentary evidence about Roman communities in England suggests that there were perhaps three towns of that name in the British Isles, the best substantiated being the one sometimes called Navimago Regnentium, now universally accepted as being at or near

Chichester, Sussex, and no doubt allied to the splendid Roman palace newly uncovered at Fishbourne. But the one named in Iter II of the *Antonine Itinerary*—that is the list which gives all the stations and their distances from one another on the route from Hadrian's Wall to the English Channel—shows Noviomagus as ten miles from London on the Kent road, eighteen miles from Vagniacae (a place now identified with the Roman remains at Springhead, near Gravesend), and twenty-seven miles from Durobrivae, the Roman name for Rochester.

Other versions of the *Itinerary*, which leave out the intermediate stations, give the distance from London to Rochester as twenty-seven miles in all. So there is an obvious discrepancy here. To account for the difference in the two sets of Roman figures, either the road must have had a diversion to take in Noviomagus or (and this is much more likely) confusion between X and V had occurred in one or more of the many copies; perhaps a copyist, finding an apparent mistake in arithmetic, sought to rectify what he did not understand and thereby added to an initial obscurity. The distance from London to Rochester in the English statute mile, slightly longer than the Roman *mille passus* which was about 1,680yd, is twenty-nine miles, and the Roman total, to be accurate, would be not twenty-seven but something nearer thirty-two—which does leave a discrepancy of five.

The realisation that Noviomagus was 'lost', and the imprecise nature of the evidence concerning it, produced a host of antiquarians anxious to discover it for themselves. William Camden was one of those who ignored the fact that it was on the Dover Road and, along with Robert Talbot and one or two others, placed it at or near Croydon: the precise site favoured by those who supported this location eventually being fixed at the neighbouring hamlet of Woodcote. William Somner put it at Crayford—on the Roman road, certainly, but too far from London. Dr Plot, a man full of Roman theories, plumped for Caesar's Camp at Keston, a choice which became so respectable in the 1820s that it gave rise to the Noviomagian Society, formed to celebrate the discovery by the antiquarians A. J. Kemp and T. Crofton Croker of substantial Roman remains there.

But Keston is too far from London in either English or Roman miles and, much more serious, no link has been discovered there with the Roman road to the coast. Nevertheless, the loyalties of its members to the idea of Keston as Noviomagus sustained the society until the discoveries at Greenwich.

One building does not make a city; and Herbert Jones's excavations could not, of course, prove a Noviomagian theory. But in those heady days at the start of the twentieth century Roman discovery was in the air; and it was assumed, at least by the amateurs, that hard work could uncover everything. A. D. Webster reported some other objects found in the park in the winter of 1901–2, including pieces of Roman and early-British pottery, and a falx or Roman pruning hook. He also described some very old water pipes dug up on the west side, near Crooms Hill. They were tapering, $4\frac{1}{2}$ft long, with a diameter at base of 9in and at top of 5in, the bore being $2\frac{1}{2}$in in diameter. They were cast, he thought, the composition being cement with pieces of stone and finely ground tile. As readers will recognise, this is a Roman mixture.

Herbert Jones and another local antiquary, J. M. Stone, set to work with a nucleus of fellow-enthusiasts to collate all the information so far gathered, with a view to promoting further investigations; and on 28 November 1905 the Greenwich Antiquarian Society was formed. The discovery most longed for by the society's members was the precise route through Greenwich of the Roman road from Canterbury to London. Its site was easily traceable from Rochester, over Shooters Hill to the Royal Standard, a public house some half a mile east of the park. It then petered out in a series of shaky and inexplicable diversions over the high ground of Blackheath. It was perfectly plain to see where it *should* have gone; one only needed to take a ruler and

align it on the known course of the road, from Shooters Hill to
the crossing of the Thames at Westminster, to see that it must
have cut across the north-east corner of the park, less than fifty
yards from the Roman building. There were even clues to its
exact position; J. M. Stone, President of the Greenwich Antiquarian Society in 1912–13, came across a document in the
Public Record Office which referred to an old road closed by
Humphrey, Duke of Gloucester, in 1433 when he fenced in the
present Greenwich Park.

The length of the closed section of the road was given as 136
perches (748yd), and another member of the society, J. E. G.
de Montmorency, went so far as to pace out this closed section
in terms of the unchanged park boundaries. It accorded exactly
with the supposed line of the lost Watling Street.

To understand the mysteries of Greenwich history, it is necessary to trace back the intricacies of the site so far as we know it.
The layout of the royal park as it is today was commissioned by
Charles II from Louis XIV's gardener André Le Nôtre, the
actual planting being done under the jurisdiction of Sir William
Boreman during the years 1662–5. How much levelling was done
to those parts of the park away from the great vista framing the
Queen's House is not certain, but the strangely shaped mounds
among which the Roman villa has been located appear to have
been left undisturbed. However, it is virtually sure that the
planting of at least one of the great elms used for the construction
of Le Nôtre's avenues must have broken into one of the tessellated floors uncovered 250 years later by Herbert Jones. Whether
this discovery was ignored through lack of awareness of its significance or because of a determination that nothing should
impede the re-establishment of Greenwich as a place of royal
residence it is impossible to say. But one wonders how many
other things were discovered, and kept quiet about, by the royal
tree-planters.

Certainly Greenwich has had an air of rumour, mystery,

supposition about it for an unusually long time, as if the local people nearly remembered some conclusive fact about the place. There is, for instance, the unresolved question of the burial ground, in the park on its western side. Although the presence of a large number of graves, some of them coffin inhumations, has been known about for hundreds of years, no official investigation has ever been carried out. Only a quarter of a mile away, under the next hill, there is the dark and sinister Blackheath Cavern, where at some unspecified (but ancient) time seven roomy chambers and a well were hacked out of the chalk by men who used antlers for tools. There are (or were—they collapsed in the 1880s) dene holes, man-made, on the heath. There are all the rounds and rectangles, against the grain of anything visible on the ground, that show up in certain aerial photographs of the park. There is the small stone well, lately uncovered in Stockwell Street and almost identical with those Roman first-century ones unearthed in Wroxeter in 1912. Above all, there is the mystery of the tunnels.

How many visitors to Greenwich realise that 40ft or more beneath their feet there is an elaborate system of inter-communicating passages? Many theories have been put forward as to the purpose of these tunnels—some undoubtedly true. They have a valuable drainage function; without them the park as we know it would scarcely exist, since the water collected in the Blackheath pebble beds would come out in soggy channels and make the lower levels marshy and unusable. One might even go further and say that without some similar drainage system the riverside town of Greenwich could not have been constructed. Here and there, in the last few years, wet patches have appeared in the park, almost certainly as a result of some ancient tunnel collapsing within the hill.

It is also certain that the water collected in these tunnels was used to supply the Tudor palace—running water being one of the perquisites of a royal dwelling. Sir Christopher Wren used some of the existing conduits for this purpose when he built Greenwich Hospital (he pronounced others, which he sealed off, as 'very ancient'); and the builders of Duke Humphrey's palace in 1433 conveyed water by this means to the ducal apartments and the kitchens.

But that the tunnels, or at least some of them, were there before, cannot be disputed. The abbot of Ghent, to whom the manor of Greenwich had been given by Elstrudis, daughter of Alfred the Great, in 918, made repairs to the tunnels as part of the maintenance of his property; among the Greenwich papers in the archives at Ghent is a bill for tunnel repairs dated 1268— nearly two hundred years before Humphrey's palace was thought of.

What exactly was bestowed by Elstrudis in her gift to the Flemish abbey is scarcely now ascertainable. But there are references in medieval documents to a great house by the river, often described as the Old Court. What is sure is that when she made the benefaction to the abbey at Ghent, Elstrudis bestowed something that was in good order and proper maintenance, and that the tunnels, since they were included, must have been there, and working, in 918.

The Anglo-Saxons were strangers to the brick-making art, and never aspired in any case to engineering works on the Roman scale. So one is forced to ask the question: who, before the Norman Conquest, had the capacity, let alone the will, to build such an elaborate water and drainage system? And for what purpose between 405 and 918 could it possibly have been conceived?

For our knowledge of the excavations at the building now known as the villa in Greenwich Park we are dependent on the accounts of A. D. Webster and Herbert Jones. We know it was discovered on a misty afternoon in February 1902; but each man gives a different date. The difference is not great—Webster mentions 6 February, Jones gives 3 February—but minor discrepancies of a similar kind are present throughout their two accounts. Much more troublesome, it is obvious from the tone of the two stories that each thought the other was making the correct archaeological notes that were essential if the excavation was to have value. Thus, while Webster includes in his book, *Greenwich Park,* a list of coins and other objects unearthed, his account of the trenching and digging is purely conversational.

Jones wrote an equally conversational account in the *Home Counties Magazine,* vol V, in which he referred to Webster as 'the director of the work of research throughout', although Webster had conveyed, and it was certainly understood locally, that Jones was the man in charge.

How the building was unearthed at all remains one of the greatest mysteries. We know from Jones that the impetus came from Webster; as superintendent he had an unrivalled knowledge of the park, and his book gives the impression that he knew more than he set down. Perhaps, too, he was influenced by that air, compounded of rumour, local legend and stubborn belief which hangs like a mist above some old places and is so noticeable at Greenwich—a kind of folk memory not scientifically measurable and seldom acknowledged by modern archaeologists, although few if any successful digs have been carried through without it.

If, for Webster, the finding of the Roman remains was an expected climax, it was soon enough followed by anti-climax. For some unaccountable reason—the discovery by either Jones or Webster that no proper record had been kept?—the excavation limped to a halt. Jones speaks in his first *Home Counties Magazine* article of more investigations to be made in the autumn. But the autumn seems to have passed without further discovery, and by 10 February 1903 the workings had been filled and turfed over, though not before everything of possible interest had been removed.

Because of the lack of notes, it is difficult to trace the exact course of the dig. But Jones describes the first finds as being only some 18in below the top of the mound. Webster gives a depth of 'hardly 2ft'. Three floors were uncovered, one of them about 14ft by 12ft. The one piece of wall found *in situ*, built, according to Jones, direct upon the Thanet sand without foundations, was at a depth of about 4ft below the surface. Jones later stated: 'The tops of the surrounding knolls were also thoroughly searched by trenching for Roman or any other remains, but without result. As on the south of the site, the undisturbed gravel or sand was always at a very short distance under the turf.'

This seems to indicate that the 'very thorough search' extended only until the diggers reached sand. But that this assessment of sand as virgin soil is—or could be—incorrect is borne out by other investigations carried out by the Greenwich Antiquarian Society.

At various times during the next twenty-five years members of this society made searches both for further traces of Roman buildings and for the ever elusive Watling Street. In 1925, for instance, the society's *Transactions* records that trial holes had been dug in various parts of the park. 'On the mound opposite the Roman villa Roman pottery was found, and some way at the back of the Roman villa *at a depth of three or four feet below what looked like virgin soil* considerable quantities of rough pottery which could not be identified as Roman were found.' The italics are mine, for these were the mounds which had been 'thoroughly searched' by Jones in 1902.

In 1927 it was recorded in the *Transactions* that three excavations had been made during the previous winter. Their purpose was to locate the line of the Roman road. One trench was dug on the east flank of the villa mound, the other two on the north; all three excavations yielded tesserae and pieces of pottery—although the Jones investigators of 1902–3 had purported to remove everything of interest turned up at that time. The 1927 findings, we are told, 'were fairly near the surface'. For some reason which must remain a mystery, no probe appears to have been made on the line paced out by J. E. G. de Montmorency.

One more note may be taken from the *Transactions*. In 1906 the Greenwich Antiquarian Society had placed funds at Mr Jones's disposal for an excavation into one of the ancient tunnels; for it had been observed, not without excitement, that this tunnel ended below the mound in which were discovered the Roman remains. Jones's findings were, in his own words, 'inconclusive'. Perhaps a clue can be found in the memorial note written at his death by his friend and colleague, Montmorency: 'He was slow to make or adopt deductions from facts and was content, very often, with accumulating carefully authenticated material for the use of other investigators.'

And Noviomagus? The one thing about the lost city which cannot be argued away is that it was on the Roman road from London to Rochester. The site of this road as it came through Greenwich had long been a matter for conjecture, and not only among members of the Greenwich Antiquarian Society. Although most historians would agree that it can be brought with reasonable precision up from Rochester, over the summit of Shooters Hill to the Standard roundabout, some half a mile eastward of the Vanbrugh Gate of Greenwich Park, after this point there is considerable divergence of opinion. It is from here that the Ordnance Survey map of Roman Britain shows the probable course of the Roman road as an uncertain dotted curve which takes us away from the straight, along the path of the present-day road over Blackheath, down Blackheath Hill to an eventual joining up with the Old Kent Road at New Cross. Local compilers of Roman data have argued quite passionately that the meandering, indeterminate nature of this part of the road was dictated by the Romans' need to avoid any possibility of their route, as it approached the capital, travelling through marshy or floodable land. But even the most cursory examination of Roman roads in other parts of their empire shows that, however they may have deflected round natural barriers in remote country, ways approaching towns were surveyed to run straight, and did so. Nor was there any problem, for Roman engineers, about building a causeway if the ground had in fact been marshy.

But people who argue that the road must have avoided the waterlogged riverside are ignoring that great natural disaster (hardly as yet investigated but of which there is a wealth of evidence) that swept a huge wall of water up the Thames Estuary, destroyed island communities at the Nore, buried under a 12ft mass of mud the eastward riverside settlements, and permanently altered the riparian landscape below London from a wooded and stable-banked valley to a muddy tidal delta. The date of this vast natural disaster is not known. It came after the start of the Roman occupation of Britain, since Roman remains have been among those found under the layer of mud. Samuel Pepys is one of the recorders who describe an effect of it: a nut tree, still with its crop of nuts, found 12ft below the ground, which he was fetched to see during the excavations for one of the royal docks at Blackwall. (So we know that the disaster was an autumnal one, and may suspect the equinoctial gales as at least adding to the cause.)

What is clear is that after this disaster the road to the north-west must of necessity have had to be re-routed on higher ground. And eastward it ceased to be of much use as a highway from the day that Humphrey, Duke of Gloucester, threw his park fence across it in 1433.

But when the Romans arrived in Britain neither of these impediments was present; and it is worth considering the military implications of the way through Greenwich Park in geographical terms. This is the point at which the surrounding hills come nearest to the Thames; where, therefore, the greatest command can be kept over both road and water. This is the one line, also, by which the road can touch the river twice—once on the Greenwich loop and again at Westminster, where we know there was a ford. Equally interesting, by following this straight line the invading legions would cross their greatest natural obstacle, the river Ravensbourne, at the point most readily defensible—that is, the narrow spit of land between the two rivers, where the parent Thames would defend their right flank.

In the arguments raging about the possibility of the road running through the park, it had long been stated that the supposed route, to the west of the steepsided One Tree Hill, would have had too severe a gradient for heavy military traffic, and that this was one of the reasons for the divergence over Blackheath. But this theory proved fallacious. The road, when found, went (as Montmorency had said it would) to the *east* of One Tree Hill, on the one path in the whole area where the gradient was easy.

It may come as a surprise to those people interested in Roman London to learn that the road (perhaps one should qualify and say *a* road) has at last been found. In the autumn of 1965 the South Eastern Gas Board decided to lay a new main; and for that purpose a trench 5ft deep and 4ft wide was cut right across Blackheath and down through Greenwich Park, within a few feet of its eastern wall—a trench which somewhere along its length must have cut across the Roman road if that road were there. By the time the trench had reached the Vanbrugh Gate those who thought the road would have passed down the gully to the west of One Tree Hill knew they were mistaken.

And then, suddenly, it was there: a disturbance in the pattern of the soil, consisting of a great ellipse of large and small gravel, like the painted smile on the face of a clown. It was about 4ft thick at its deepest point, and some twenty-five yards wide— one must remember that the trench would cut across the road at an angle, but Ivan Margary, in that evocative book, *Roman Roads in Britain*, describes a number of major routes as being 75ft or 80ft in width—and, for the record, it was within a yard of the point of entry indicated by J. E. G. de Montmorency.

If the Romans used the Thames at Greenwich—and common-sense suggests that they must at least have wanted to—one would expect to find a dock at the point where the road skirted the water. In fact, traces of such a dock, called Billingsgate and situated a few yards to the west of the pier, have long been known to Greenwich antiquarians. One may also take note of that very old Greenwich thoroughfare with the thought-provoking name of Straightsmouth, still existing in part, which ran down from Greenwich High Road to the exact point where Montmorency's Watling Street, the dock and the Thames all met.

Although not enough evidence has yet accrued to make a firm statement about Noviomagus possible, it should also be recorded that a later SEGAS trench dug at the start of 1971 from east to west of the park on about the centre line revealed traces of two other ancient roads. One of them was unquestionably of Roman construction, the characteristic ditch and the layered gravel being plainly seen; this skirted the north-west foot of Observatory Hill, and ran on a line that would take it from Ballast Quay up towards the burial ground, on what appeared to be an exact diagonal to the park stretch of Watling Street. The second road, less precise in foundation, was on the same parallel and seemed to link up with the broad track, still visible on the surface, that rises diagonally up the north face of the part of Crooms Hill which lies within the park.

Although an examination of the Roman situation at Greenwich solves some of the mysteries, there are undoubtedly others which it raises. For the reason why the Roman invaders should select this point for a river termination of their first and most important road unquestionably depended upon what was there before. And the evidence is all but inescapable that here was a crossing into the lands we now call Essex.

The main path of the Thames, uncorrupted as yet by that great flood already referred to, lay probably in much the same bed as today. But the low-lying banks must have had a very different look; some of the overthrown trees have been found to have a maturity of several hundred years. Even in the nineteenth century, when it had not been appreciated that the disaster might have been a sudden and overwhelming one, geologists realised from the depth of the London Roman levels that the water must have been of much less extent and much shallower. There was also no evidence that it had been tidal. We know from remains that the Romans built on ground which later would have been impossible because of its soggy nature; but that there was some marsh near London is proved by descriptions of the Roman invasions of both Caesar and Claudius. There was also, somewhere, a ford.

The tidal end of the river, the point at which it might first be fordable, would be the ideal spot for settlement, not only locally but as a geographical focus for the country over a wide area. And no more for the Romans than for those shadowy people who preceded them. It would seem absurd at this stage of history, here in the last years of the twentieth century, to look for unsifted evidence that so ancient and important a site might be found at Greenwich. Yet, there is an amazing quantity of material, both written and archaeological, that supports this theory.

Accounts of pre-Roman Britain are not quite so flimsy as the popular idea would lead us to believe, although it is true that Caesar's description, factual and assertive, in Book V of *De Bello Gallico* is accurate only in terms of what a soldier needs to know for his campaign. Some of the assumptions, such as that everyone wore woad and groups of ten or twelve men shared wives in common, are likely to have been superficial if not mistaken—the usual highly coloured impressions of an unknown enemy.

Caesar described the people of Kent as by far the most civilised of the country (though how did he know, since his personal experience did not extend much beyond that county?). That they were considerably mature we can see from their artefacts. And the picture he painted—of a race of tillers of the soil; an immense population; prosperous homesteads at every turn; numerous cattle; and a currency of gold and iron—fits well with the other, more detailed sources of information that we have.

Factual contemporary writers on pre-Roman Britain can be numbered on the fingers; almost without exception they are outsiders—travellers from Europe. Our richest pool of knowledge comes from Wales, where the chroniclers, direct descendants of the pre-Roman English, are nevertheless writing, even the earliest of them, some hundreds of years after the events they describe.

Some of their primary sources may have been written; more must have been passed down by word of mouth. But verbal history, transmitted in a formal, impersonal and stylised way as it undoubtedly was, would be very little less reliable than the written record; and though a proud and ancient people, anxious to retain the memory of their origins, would obviously present incidents in the light most favourable to themselves, there is no adequate reason to disbelieve accounts of the past because they are unsupported by the force of pen on paper.

After Caesar's own enthralling but regrettably untopographical account, the other sources of ancient history scarcely range beyond Gildas, Nennius and Geoffrey of Monmouth. That great work the *Anglo-Saxon Chronicle* was, as its name implies, an attempt by the post-Roman, post-British conquerors of England to enshrine their own origins in permanent form.

Both Gildas, writing perhaps about 540, and Nennius, flourishing some 300 years later, gave only a cursory glance to the time before the coming of the Romans. Gildas contented himself with describing its prosperity and its heathenism; Nennius, quoting from 'the ancient books of our ancestors', gave a coherent narrative of the arrival of one, Brutus, from Troy and the founding of the British nation. It was left to Geoffrey of Monmouth in the 1130s to produce a work which purported to give a factual and detailed account of these people. According to his own description, Geoffrey's source was a book brought out of Brittany—that first British colony—in the British (ie Welsh) tongue, which he did little more than translate into Latin. But there is evidence that he also set down a number of the spoken histories.

Although his narrative thread is similar in general terms to that of Nennius, and can be corroborated in many important details by historical remains or chronicles from continental sources, Geoffrey's tale contains a number of allegories and examples of wishful thinking on the part of the ancient storytellers that the fact-loving Victorians could not stomach. And during the nineteenth century it became the historical fashion to dismiss virtually the whole of Geoffrey's work as valueless legend.

The modern study of psychology has given us an insight into why men choose such words as they do, why they stress this incident and gloss over that. In the first century BC, the Stoic philosopher Posidonius wrote of the Celts: 'They go in much for exaggeration in talk, with the aim of glorifying themselves and belittling others.' It becomes easier today than it has ever been to separate the *Historia Regum Britanniae*'s wheat from its chaff.

And one of the chief reasons for discarding Geoffrey's work as insubstantial fancy was an error due not to himself at all; an error which, once corrected, makes a re-reading of all his account little short of obligatory.

Geoffrey stated that Brutus and his followers, after many European adventures (and in a period later, though probably incorrectly, calculated as about 1100 BC), finished his journey from Troy by landing in Britain, which he found uninhabited except for a few giants. After the initial stage of disembarkation and establishment, he set about to build his capital. He chose, as any sensible newcomer would, the Thames; walking along the shore, he 'at last pitched upon a place very fit for his purpose', and there erected the fine and beautiful city of Trinovantum. It did not occur to the readers of Geoffrey of Monmouth, nor apparently to those of any of his post-Roman predecessors, that a Thames capital of England could be other than London.

Geoffrey, indeed, gives an account of the changing of the name from Trinovantum to Lud-town, and so to London, by Lud, brother of Julius Caesar's opponent, Cassivellaunus—an act which caused serious quarrels among those Britons who wished the ancient origin of their city to be remembered. Geoffrey adds the significant detail that an account of all this is more fully written about by Gildas—although search through the writings of both Gildas and Nennius as they have come down to us fails to find any such account. The halting nature of his phrases suggests that there is a gap in his own information here —a glimpse of some old document wrongly remembered, perhaps; a page of manucript torn; a phrase mistranslated. For although London might believably have been founded a year or two before the first invasion of Caesar, all the accounts of the much more ancient city of Trinovantum show that it could not have been where London is. The archaeological evidence also denies its presence there; virtually no prehistoric remains have been uncovered. But we are not left with a blank. All the documentary evidence, and all the archaeological evidence too, supports a contention that Trinovantum was at Greenwich.

From the very beginning the scene is set here, in this place, among geographical features that are still identifiable: the river on its golden strand; the settlement set on flat ground at the foot of steep-sided hills; the wooded combes reaching up into the hinterland. (In one of these combes the wicked king Mempricius, great-grandson of Brutus, was devoured by wolves 'in a horrible manner'.)

Brutus was succeeded by his son Locrin, and soon afterwards the young warrior king fell in love with Estrildis, a German girl captured along with other booty from the king of the Huns. Estrildis 'had beauty such as was hardly to be matched. No ivory or new-fallen snow, no lily could exceed the whiteness of her

skin.' Locrin wished to marry Estrildis; but he was already engaged to Gwendolina, daughter of his father's old ally, Corineus,
king of Cornwall. Corineus forces Locrin to honour his engage-
ment and make Gwendolina his queen. But, 'resolved at least to
carry on a private amour', Locrin causes a great underground
cavern to be made for Estrildis, 'since he could not live with her
openly for fear of Corineus. In this manner he concealed her, and
made frequent visits to her for seven years together, without the
privity of any but his most intimate domestics; and all under a
pretence of performing some secret sacrifice to his gods.'

Most residents, and many visitors, will have heard of the vast
Greenwich cave known as the Blackheath Cavern, of great antiquity and unknown use, hacked out of the chalk by tools made
of antler, under that curiously terraced spur of Blackheath now
called Point Hill; four large and three small chambers; a well at
its farthest end; a Celtic carving of a devil-god just within its
entrance.

Many vignettes of life at Trinovantum can be quarried out of
Geoffrey's book, with geographical details that fit a Greenwich
he did not know. There was Bladud, the necromancer, founder
of Bath and father of Shakespeare's King Lear. He was something of an aeronaut, and from a height above the city, easily
equated with the steep-faced One Tree Hill, on the east side of
Greenwich Park, 'he attempted to fly to the upper region of the
air with wings which he had prepared, and fell down upon the
temple of Apollo in the city of Trinovantum, where he was
dashed to pieces.'

There were the building kings, Dunwallo Molmutius and
Belinus his son. Belinus, whose brother Brennius marched on
Rome in 390 BC and sacked it, is credited with building the
ancient roads of which the so-called Pilgrim's Way is the best
known to ourselves. He 'made a gate of wonderful structure in
Trinovantum, on the banks of the Thames, which the citizens
call after his name Billingsgate to this day. Over it he built a

prodigiously large tower, and under it a haven or quay for ships.' Geoffrey assumed, as many another historian has done, that Billingsgate meant London. But at Greenwich there is another Billingsgate which, besides being older, is more precisely placed for this account, with a dock at its river end, and the hill, long the site of a tower, where Greenwich Observatory now stands, rising like the prow of a ship above it.

The frequent mention of the Tower of Trinovantum was particularly troubling to Geoffrey's editors, who, having no suspicion that it might be elsewhere, tried vainly to equate it with the Tower of London and then chided the *Historia* for putting it in the wrong time and the wrong place. What Trinovantum Tower was like we can only guess at. But it must have been strong and reasonably roomy; it provided a prison for, among others, the pious King Elidure, persecuted by his ambitious brothers and locked away in it for seven years.

It seems also to have been used as the royal mausoleum; a number of kings of Trinovantum are said to be buried there. After Belinus's death (and Geoffrey gets the burial customs right, though twelfth-century writers had little or no archaeological knowledge) his ashes were 'put up in a golden urn, which they placed at Trinovantum with wonderful art on the top of the tower'.

Thirty-four kings after Elidure we come to Caesar's times, and that King Lud who is credited with founding London. It is the identification of his work at Greenwich that concerns us here; he rebuilt the walls of Trinovantum, earlier raised by Belinus, 'which he also surrounded with innumerable towers. He likewise commanded the citizens to build houses and all other kinds of structures, so that no city in all foreign countries to a great distance round could show more beautiful palaces.'

The walled city, familiar to us in many still-standing examples throughout Europe, was not a concept of prehistoric Britain. The British *oppidum* (the name given it by the Romans) was a straggling place; both Camulodunum (Colchester) and Cassivel-launus's city near St Albans covered miles rather than acres. But adjoining these scattered townships was the fortified place, generally a grass-covered hill banked by huge earth ramparts and protected by stakes and thorn thickets, into which the city's inhabitants and their livestock could be gathered while a battle raged. Thus, strengthening the walls of Trinovantum meant reinforcing the nearby place of shelter for the citizens, inhabitants of those Thames-side villas and palaces referred to by Lud, and the farmers and the artisans of the town.

Can we look for any archaeological evidence at Greenwich in support of this description? Is there such a stronghold within a practicable distance of this site? Nothing of the kind has ever been discovered in London.

Down river, a little more than a mile to the east of Greenwich, lie the earthworks of Charlton. That Charlton was an ancient British strongpoint of considerable extent was first seriously proposed by Sir Flinders Petrie in 1870; and some thorough and very valuable researches were carried out over subsequent years by the local antiquarian, F. C. Elliston-Erwood. These investigations had no difficulty at all in proving that there had been a fortified hill settlement at Charlton for many centuries, $17\frac{1}{2}$ acres in extent, the earth walls considerably amplified and reconstructed about the middle of the first century BC, the whole stronghold perhaps originating in the Early Iron Age. Almost all this hill has been excavated away for its sand; Maryon Park now occupies the floor of the quarry thus left; but on the west spur which remains, there is still a wild, tangled thicket of a kind that might well have deterred an invader.

F. C. Elliston-Erwood would have liked to equate this British settlement with the Roman town of Noviomagus. But though a number of Romano-British relics have turned up at Charlton, showing that the local people continued to occupy their defensive stronghold for some four hundred years after the Romans arrived, no evidence has been discovered that the armies of Rome came to the place, either to do battle or to live. What seems to have been an abrupt end to the occupation fits in well, on the other hand, with the *Anglo-Saxon Chronicle* account of Hengist's victory at Crayford in 456, when the Britons 'fled in great fear to London'.

Can we seek any corroboration from *De Bello Gallico* for a Greenwich Trinovantum? Caesar, too, turns out to be a substantial supporting witness. Shortly before his first invasion, Geoffrey of Monmouth tells us, King Lud died and should have been succeeded by his two young sons, Tenuantius and Androgeus. But Cassivellaunus, who was their uncle, thought they were too young to hold the kingdom. This dispossession of minors is a custom carried down well past the Norman Conquest.

To compensate them for their lost inheritance, Cassivellaunus 'bestowed the city of Trinovantum, with the dukedom of Kent, on Androgeus'. To Tenuantius he gave the dukedom of Cornwall. Androgeus is, of course, that young prince of the Trinovantes whom Caesar called Mandubracius. And we might remember, when we examine the evidence concerning the unmolested state of the British settlement at Charlton, that Caesar ordered his own troops, as well as those of Cassivellaunus, to leave Mandubracius and the Trinovantes alone.

Mandubracius's brother, Tenuantius, who succeeded to the throne on Cassivellaunus's death (he himself choosing to remain in Rome), is better known as that Tasciovanus under whose son Cunobelinus the territories of the Catuvellauni and the Trinovantes became firmly united. Who it was who first placed the Trinovantian name on the Essex bank of the Thames to the exclusion of their Kent holding I do not know. (The Egyptian mathematician and geographer, Ptolemy, writing about AD 135, did so, and it was right for his time that they should have expanded northward. He ignored the fact that they were still in occupation at Greenwich—or Charlton—though what his sources of information were we cannot be sure; it is worth noting that he put Londinium on the south bank of the Thames.)

This is not, unfortunately, the place to examine the question as to whether Greenwich was the scene of either Caesar's crossing of the Thames or that of Claudius in AD 43. Of course there have been many arguments in favour of crossings higher up. But a pre-flood Thames, here fordable, fits well with contemporary accounts of both Roman invasions. Opposite Greenwich the river Lea, often quoted as the western boundary of Trinovantian territory, could also provide a quick and direct route to the stronghold of Cassivellaunus. At that time the Isle of Dogs was almost certainly a tidally inundated marsh, while on the southern bank of the Thames there is that tongue of Greenwich marsh, now drained, which extended landward right to the heel of the British strong-point at Charlton. It was Nennius, not Geoffrey of Monmouth, who wrote that Julius Caesar defeated the Britons 'near a place called Trinovantum'; and the first-century historian, Cassius Dio, who described the loss of Claudian troops in a marsh while following the British across the Thames 'at a point near where it empties into the ocean and at flood tide forms a lake'.

Antoninus Pius, who gave his name to the Antonine Itinerary. Several coins of his reign (AD 138–161) were found at the villa in the park

CHAPTER 2

The Kings of Kent

After 405, the Dark Ages. It was as if the last Roman, marching down Watling Street to embarkation and the transports home, pulled over his shoulder a huge, black, all-enveloping curtain. The resulting gloom is as great in Greenwich as in other parts of Britain; but in Kent generally, where the folds had last been dragged over, they were also the most easily lifted. So it is from this south-east corner of England that the historical light first starts to seep back.

Some time after the last Roman had left, a band of Europeans, led by the brothers Hengist and Horsa, landed at Ebbsfleet, near Pegwell Bay. They were men spoiling for a fight, mercenaries, and their employer and paymaster was to be Vortigern, King of Kent, and probably king of much more of Britain. The date has been variously given as between 420 and 450; it seems likely to have been about 448. We owe most of our knowledge about Vortigern to Geoffrey of Monmouth; and in spite of the Victorian dismissal of Geoffrey's account as legend, there is no doubt that Vortigern was a real person. Nennius wrote of him, and Gildas, and Bede; but Geoffrey's account is the fullest.

Vortigern, says Geoffrey, was a prince of the Gewissi—a territory later to be considered as Wessex. And he gained the crown by arranging for the killing of Constans, who was then wearing it. Constans had two young brothers, who after the murder were hurried by their friends overseas to Brittany, out of the usurper's way. Their names were Aurelius Ambrosius and Uther Pendragon—and Arthurians will recognise in the latter the man who was to become King Arthur's father.

Hengist and Horsa (Horsus, as Geoffrey prefers to call him) appeared off the Kent coast with three longboats filled with armed warriors, one day while Vortigern was visiting Canterbury. He summoned the strangers to his presence—'certain men unknown and big of stature'—and asked them their business. According to Geoffrey, they described themselves as Saxons, and explained that they had been banished from their own country because of over-population difficulties, the laws of inheritance, and the lack of land for younger sons to succeed to. Vortigern thereupon engaged them to beat back the Picts who were at that time harassing the northern provinces, and, after victory had been gained, offered as a reward various territories for settlement.

The immigrants now sent back to Germany for their dependants; eighteen shiploads of warriors were included among the retinue but, more important for Vortigern, Hengist's daughter Rowen came too, a girl of such great beauty that 'his heart was enkindled of delight', to quote the usually more restrained Geoffrey. The scene is described at which Hengist invited Vortigern to his house, entertained him to a 'banquet royal', and afterwards motioned forth Rowen, who came from her chamber bearing a golden cup filled with wine, approached the king and knelt before him, saying: 'Lord King, wassail!' To which Vortigern was told the custom was to reply 'Drink Heil!' He gave the response, and kissed her. This simple ceremony was repeated over and over again. Whereupon, Geoffrey tells us, 'Vortigern, drunken with the divers kinds of liquor, Satan entering his heart, did wax enamoured of the damsel, and demanded her of her father.'

Bede has the account more briefly. The foreign warriors were called in by Vortigern to help him secure the country against the Picts, in about 450. As a reward for their help they were given Thanet. Gradually they spread outwards, and ultimately acquired all Kent. Bede also makes the significant statement that they were Jutes—significant because one of the obscurities of Kentish history lies in the fact that some of her laws, and notably those of inheritance, are different, certain customs such as gavel-kind arising not from Anglo-Saxon law, nor apparently from Celtic, but from some source unknown. William the Conqueror recognised the peculiar nature of 'the common law of Kent' and allowed it to stand.

There seems no reason to doubt that Vortigern and Rowen were married, or that the favour shown by the besotted king to his wife's relations became increasingly irksome to his own subjects. According to Geoffrey, Vortigern was a Christian; and it was as much the heathen practices of Hengist and his people which enraged the Britons as the fact that more and more foreign warriors were pouring into the country.

Vortigern had been married before; and at last the Britons went to his three sons, Vortimer, Katigern and Pascentius, and asked them to take up arms against the barbarians. In a battle near Aylesford, says Geoffrey, where Horsus and Katigern met hand to hand, each mortally wounded the other. Bede tells us Horsa was slain by Vortigern. Whichever version is right, there is little doubt that shortly before 455 the Britons had become sufficiently roused to turn on the interlopers and send them back to Europe, Vortimer driving them down to the Isle of Thanet and into their ships.

There followed disaster for Vortimer. No sooner had he restored the Christian churches and handed back to his father's subjects their plundered lands and stolen cattle than his stepmother Rowen, archetype of such wicked women, called in a witch and had him poisoned. Vortimer died lingeringly but bravely, distributing among his soldiers the gold and silver that his forefathers 'had heaped together'. Comforting his weeping followers, he commanded that

a brazen pyramid should be wrought for him, and set in the

haven wherein the Saxons were wont to land, and that after his death his body should be buried on the top thereof, so as that when the barbarians beheld his image thereupon they should back sail and turn them home again to Germany. For he said that not one of them durst come anigh so they did even behold his image. O, the passing great hardihood of the man who was thus desirous that even after death he might be dreaded by those unto whom while living he had been a terror! But after his death the Britons did otherwise, for they buried his corpse in the city of Trinovantum.

The name sticks out like a thorn in the thumb; for this is post-Roman chronicling, four hundred years after the establishment of London; and it reveals that the ancient capital not only remains, but continues as the royal mausoleum.

Modern students of history know much more about Hengist than Geoffrey of Monmouth could possibly have known; it is one of the great excitements of his narrative that details crop up the significance of which he could not have appreciated. After Vortimer's death Hengist returned to Kent, Vortigern and Rowen welcoming him; presumably he came to the old capital. Victorian anthropologists went to work on the Jutes, whose European country of origin has been fairly conclusively narrowed down to Friesland, a northern province of the Netherlands which then reached up to the borders of Denmark. The Frisian physical type was, said John Beddoe, author of *The Races of Britain*, 'an extremely fair and very comely people'. They were taller, he said, longer in the face, more universally blond and blue-eyed than the Saxons. They were slenderly built, oval-faced with flat cheekbones; their long noses were straight or aquiline; their chins well developed, their skins very fair. John Beddoe was writing in 1885; but all the nineteenth-century anthropologists agreed that this physical type, found in south-east England and the Isle of Wight, where it is known the Jutes had a colony, was particularly prevalent in the north-west of Kent.

There comes an odd corroboration of Geoffrey of Monmouth's perhaps involuntary picture of fifth-century Trinovantum. In 1779 a man obsessed with antiquity, the Rev James Douglas, came to the conclusion that

> by contemplating the relics discovered in our ancient sepultures, the historian may have an opportunity of comparing them with similar relics found in different places. . . . If a medal or inscription be found in a sepulchre . . . the undoubted characteristic of the customs of a people at the time of the deposit, and the superscription on the medal or the inscription evincing a low period, it will be a self-evident position that similar relics under similar forms of sepulture, discovered in other parts of the island, cannot apply to a period more remote.

Those raised conical mounds known as tumuli were mentioned by Richard of Cirencester, writing in the fourteenth century, as 'the graves of the Britons'. Geoffrey of Monmouth describes them too, but tells us their formation was a custom of the Paynims (pagans). They are generally found on barren ground, says Douglas, on commons, moors, sometimes on parish grounds near villages. The largest seldom exceed 33ft in diameter, the smallest 13ft. He goes on: 'They are sometimes very neatly fashioned, with the circumjacent sod raised from the plane; their height was originally proportioned to their circumference; but time has compressed their cones, and in many places laid them almost level to the surface of the ground.' Douglas adds: 'They are generally furnished with a narrow trench, which seems to have been fashioned from a funereal superstitious custom . . .' Other writers have described a Jutish funeral ceremony where the mourners processed round the tumulus, chanting the deeds of the deceased.

It was on 22 January 1784 that Douglas, having obtained permission from the Hon John Pitt, Surveyor General of the Royal Domains, started his dig among the burial mounds of Greenwich

Park. He was a careful excavator; accounts of his findings are scrupulously given, and many of his descriptions are accompanied by precisely dimensioned drawings. He had looked up the somewhat scanty records of the Greenwich mounds, and had read Lambarde's opinion that they were burial sites of the Danes, who had camped on Blackheath for three years from 1011.

Douglas had already had wide experience of Dark Age burials, and his work among the tumuli at Chatham Lines and in the Anglo-Saxon cemeteries round Canterbury, worked out in conjunction with the Rev Bryan Faussett, led him to the conviction that the Greenwich Park mounds were of the same time and people. His description is particularly interesting to us, since he was looking at a site still then undamaged and complete. He records the cluster of graves as 'nearly in a circular form', about 100ft in diameter; and he gives the number of mounds as 'about fifty'. He goes on: 'The soil on which these tumuli are situated is gravel, and in some places extremely compact. The incision for the body about a foot and a half, or less, in some of them, below the surface, in the native soil; the barrow, or the conic mound of earth raised above it most probably collected from the trench, which encircles it, and from a spot of ground excavated on the East side of the range of tumuli.' This excavation to the east may still be seen today.

Douglas left fairly detailed notes of eighteen barrows which he opened. From the biggest, in the middle of the cluster, he recovered 'one of the largest iron spearheads I ever found; fifteen inches long and two broad to the socket; . . . the spear near the head; towards the centre a knife of iron, and fragments of an umbo of a shield of the same metal. No remains of bones; but on a line where the body seemed to have been laid, a considerable quantity of fine vegetable mould; probably the decomposed particles of some wooden case in which the corpse had been deposited.'

From another tumulus, which was crossed by the Crooms Hill

path and very much flattened by it, Douglas found 'a braid of human hair; the braid tenacious and very distinct; and the hair itself, which was of an auburn colour, contained its natural phlogiston'. There was some factor in the Greenwich soil, Douglas concluded, which preserved hair and fibre, while decaying bones; for many of the barrows contained, besides hair, identifiable pieces of cloth, mostly wool but also linen and silk, so perfectly preserved that the weave could be clearly seen. The grave that contained the braid of hair had been lined with woollen cloth of a herringbone pattern; there was in it the remains of a garment, and several beads similar in type to beads found at Chatham and Canterbury.

Who were these people, buried with pomp and reverence, though in the heathen manner, on a Greenwich hill above the Thames? A number of the graves he had uncovered elsewhere in Kent had yielded Douglas coins and other tokens which made close dating possible. From the Greenwich finds, the spears and the shield bosses, and 'similar beads to those [barrows] wherein I have found coins' he concluded that the graves in Greenwich Park must be among the earliest, dating to 'the fifth and beginning of the sixth century'. Unfortunately, some seventy years before his own excavations, a park-keeper named Hearne had been known to be occupying himself with extensive digging in the vicinity of the graves, and old inhabitants of Greenwich whom Douglas questioned could remember that he had recovered several things of value.

So the most vital evidence of identity had already been stolen, and we must go back and comb the chronicles to see if there is any clue to whoever might have been buried here at Greenwich.

The stilted old accounts suddenly assume an almost overwhelming significance. Hengist and Horsa land in 448. Some time after a marriage between King Vortigern and Hengist's daughter Rowen, Horsa is killed at Aylesford, in a year confirmed as 455. The Britons, led by Vortimer, chase the invaders away; Vortimer dies and is buried at Trinovantum. Perhaps at Vortigern's invitation, the invaders return; but fighting quickly breaks out again, and the Battle of Crayford, in 456, settles the history of Kent. The Britons are beaten, and flee. Reaching Salisbury, Wiltshire, Vortigern and his nobles turn for a parley with Hengist. There is a huge Anglo-Saxon treachery—the old manuscripts cry out with it—and some hundreds of the British, unarmed and unsuspecting, are done to death at a feast. Vortigern escapes to Wales; and in Geoffrey's account (after the interpolation, so distasteful to nineteenth-century historians, of the prophecies of Merlin), the story is resumed of his death at the hands of Aurelius Ambrosius, in revenge for that old murder of the latter's brother, Constans. Vortigern's end is described in more than one chronicle; he had fled with Rowen to the castle of Genoreu, in Wales, and perished within its walls when Ambrosius, having failed to take it by siege, managed to burn the tower and its occupants to ashes. Hengist then went on to rule in Kent until 488, when he was succeeded by his son Octa (sometimes called Oisc).

Vortimer is recorded as having been buried in Trinovantum. But Vortimer was a Christian, and would not have been interred under one of those conical mounds, which were the mark of the infidel. Vortigern's funeral pyre was the castle of Genoreu. So whose was that central mound in royal Greenwich, dating from the fifth century, one of the earliest of the graves, with the biggest spear that the Rev James Douglas had ever unearthed in some five hundred digs?

That Hengist died in 488 is attested in the *Anglo-Saxon Chronicle*, and both this account and that of the historian Nennius state that he was succeeded as King of Kent by his son Octa (or Oisc). Geoffrey of Monmouth provides a factual account of Hengist's death : Aurelius Ambrosius, with a vast army of the Britons of Brittany, had pursued the Saxons north beyond the Humber, where they had taken refuge. And in a great battle near Knaresborough the Britons won the day and Hengist was captured and beheaded. Octa, who had fled to York, came out to Ambrosius when he heard of his father's death, and begged for mercy. It was granted on condition that Octa retreated into Scotland.

But we know that in fact Octa returned to Kent, and ruled there. Did he bring the body of his slaughtered father with him? Could the 'considerable quantity of fine black vegetable mould, probably the decomposed particles of some wooden case in which the corpse had been deposited' as recorded by the Rev James Douglas in his excavation of the largest barrow with the biggest spear—could that have been the coffin in which the mutilated remains of their king had been brought south by the Jutes, to be buried with due ceremony in the capital of their kingdom? And can we take as any sort of confirmation of this the final word on Hengist by Geoffrey of Monmouth: 'Aurelius, that was ever sober in all things, bade him be buried, and a mound of earth be heaped above his body after the manner of the Paynims'?

The evidence, though slender, is curiously persistent: Trinovantum, the ancient capital, the place that Richard of Cirencester described as older than Rome (though London scarcely antedated Caesar); the chosen spot for the grave of Vortimer; the city whose annexation and occupation would confer the greatest prestige on a foreign usurper of the throne—in primitive times there would be many who could not assimilate a victor's triumph without seeing him in possession of the trappings of the vanquished, and Hengist, first of the invaders, would need the great palace by the river, the royal mausoleum.

Perhaps Vortimer was buried near the Thames, in that early but undated graveyard uncovered in 1860 near the tilt-yard of the Tudor palace (now the Royal Naval College car park). But the Jutes had a religion different from the ancient Christianity of their predecessors. They had to take, as was their custom, a lofty site on a bare hillside, its brow in sight of the living below. 'The boundary of a territory seems to have been the proper place for them,' writes Audrey Meaney, in her *Gazetteer of Early Anglo-Saxon Burial Sites*, 'even if that boundary were a Roman road.'

This was a small cemetery, of no more than fifty burials, although obviously very important ones. The succession of the House of Hengist is recorded by more than one of the chroniclers. Octa, after a reasonably stable reign, was succeeded by his son Eoric, whose son Eormoric had for son that Ethelbert, King of Kent, who was converted to Christianity by Augustine in 597. So Ethelbert and his successors would have been buried in the Christian manner, in graves in or near a Christian church. However slow the march of Christianity in other parts of Kent, the pagan royal burial ground on its windswept hill would be in use from Hengist's death in 488 only to the death of the last member of Ethelbert's family before his conversion.

And what about the auburn braid? Who among the Jutish women would be likely to have hair of that colour? Whose body was it that they laid in a grave sumptuously lined with woollen cloth, dressed in linen and silk, and buried with who knows what jewels removed by the park-keeper, Hearne? Not Rowen, for her hair is likely to have been flaxen. Besides, she was consumed in the flames at Genoreu. It was Vortigern's people, the Celts, who had red hair. But Vortigern was a Christian, and Christians were not buried in this fashion.

Could it have been a daughter of Vortigern and Rowen, inheriting her father's hair and her mother's religion? Or some foreign bride of Hengist's son or grandson? Ethelbert's wife, Bertha, was a Christian princess of Europe, daughter of Charibert, King of the Franks; but we do not know where his predecessors sought their brides. Could their queens have come, by some rough social justice, from the ranks of the conquered Britons?

However strategically important the placing of the prehistoric Trinovantum might have been, the Roman invasion had produced an irreversible change in Britain. For by uniting there in a peaceful continuity the territories above and below the Thames, they made London the inevitable focal point of communication between north and south. Once a stable network of roads and bridges had made this the crossing, there could be no further need of a capital city downstream. And the coming of the flood, mentioned in Chapter 1, widening and deepening the river at Greenwich where perhaps a ford had earlier been possible, took much of the geographical significance of that centre away. The very nearness of the now more importantly placed London must have contributed to its decline. And as the kingdom of Kent itself lost status, and the Christian Church, with a concentration on the two great ecclesiastical focal points of Canterbury and Rochester, began to make nonsense of the older supremacies, the community at Greenwich must have sunk down towards that condition of small fishing town described by Hasted as characteristic of its earlier days.

Scraps of history light the dark years of the seventh century. Ethelbert's daughter, the Princess Ethelburga, had married Edwin, Anglo-Saxon king of Northumbria; and in a memorable ceremony at York on Easter Day, 627, had seen him baptised a Christian by Paulinus. Six years later, at Hatfield, Yorkshire, Edwin was killed in a battle with the heathen Penda, king of Mercia; and the widowed Queen Ethelburga was escorted back to her old home in Kent by her bishop, Paulinus. They came by sea; it is tempting to think he brought her to Greenwich. But he was a monk of Canterbury, where her mother's chapel was, and his own pastoral territory was to be Rochester. We have no evidence that the sad little flotilla, the young widow and her two children, came north to the house on the Thames.

But one thing we do know. Although Ethelbert had built a palace at Canterbury (which he later handed over to Augustine, himself moving to Reculver), the royal property at Greenwich, whatever it now consisted of, still remained in royal hands.

A 19th-century engraving of Blackheath Cavern. This prehistoric cave, of one large chamber and several smaller ones, the furthest containing a well, has been lost and rediscovered several times over the centuries. It was last examined in 1946

a ▲

d ▼

b ▲

c ▼

a. Part of a statue found at the Roman villa site in Greenwich Park

b. Pottery from the villa site

c. Roofing tiles from the Roman building

d. Bronze brooch of the second century AD, decorated with silver, gold and blue enamel; found in the British stronghold at Charlton

It is an irony of this part of the history of Greenwich that so many of the things described are not written about until they are old. The accounts recorded in the chronicles are not so much eye-witness writing of contemporaneous events—a man engaged in a piece of building, a soldier's action topically acclaimed—as references to things already past, even the memory fading. Thus, the house by the river, which begins to have a positive identity in documents of the twelfth and thirteenth centuries, is by then referred to as 'the old house', 'old court', something once great but now less so. It is fortunate indeed for Greenwich historians that a ninth-century princess of England was pious and generous, and gave her dowry to the Church.

Although there is some historical confusion about the powers of the rulers of Kent after Ethelbert, it is perfectly possible to trace the royal thread of possession. Nennius gives the descent; so does the *Anglo-Saxon Chronicle*. After Ethelbert's death in 616 his son Eadbald succeeded, to be followed by his son Earconbert, and his son Egbert. There seem to have been occasional dual kings, dividing the rule of east and west Kent between them. But one, if not both, was always in the royal line. That brilliant Egbert who became the first King of England was the son of Ealhmund, himself King of Kent under the rulers of Wessex, and a descendant of Ethelbert—probably his great-great-great-great-grandson. Egbert, coming to the Wessex throne in 802, always regarded Kent as his homeland, and in 825, after pursuing the pretender, Baldred, northward across the Thames, installed his son Ethelwulf as under-king of Kent, much as later monarchs were to invest the heir to the throne as Prince of Wales. Ethelwulf, who died in 858 still King of Kent (the larger throne having been annexed by his eldest son Ethelbald), left an elaborate will in which he bestowed kingdoms, properties and palaces on his children and kinsmen. The survivor of his sons is to take all the individual bequests made to them; and by the time his youngest son Alfred succeeds his three brothers and inherits

the throne in 871, the royal manor is listed among his possessions, and the long documentation of Greenwich has begun.
It is less easy to be precise about the change of name. The
ancient city of Trinovantum was, of course, British—that is to
say, Celtic. But the name as we have it is only Latin. Possibly
the original was something like the Troynovant occasionally
given by Geoffrey of Monmouth. Apparently it was the Kent historian Edward Hasted, writing in the last years of the eighteenth
century, who first offered a Saxon derivation: Grenavic, the
'green town by the river'. But this is likely to be no more correct
than his assessment of the Greenwich of Henry V as 'a small
fishing town'. 'Grene' is Anglo-Saxon for the colour, pronounced
long, as in Greenhithe; 'wich' is Anglo-Saxon for a tree. *Vicus* is
Roman for a district of a town, which might, perhaps, be a little
nearer. But in all the early spellings the first syllable is not 'grene'
or 'green', but 'gron': Gronewic, Gronavic, Gronovic—the last
as late as Henry I. And where is the riparian reference, the
acknowledging word for what must always have been the main
feature of this place? Why no syllable for the all-important hills?
And why, above all, should a known and ancient city be given a
new name, one so indefinite and unimaginative?

Hengist, friend and ally of Vortigern before usurper, must
have known what his son-in-law called his capital. Unlike other
Anglo-Saxon conquests, this was no surprise raid on an unknown
citadel; and all that his Jutish followers changed when they took
over is likely to have been the accent of the place. The Saxon
language, according to the Normans, was like the barking of
dogs; the melodious Troynovant becomes bitten off to Tronovic,
and thus by easy stages to Gronevic—or so we may suppose.
Perhaps this occurred when Hengist's grandson, Eoric, was on
the throne, and the -ic ending was made additionally fashionable by the exploits of those contemporary raiders Cerdic and
Cynric, themselves very probably Jutes, whose conquests in
Hampshire and the Isle of Wight would certainly be known to

the conquerors of Kent.

In his *Roman Occupation*, Professor Francis Haverfield wrote: 'No case is known where Saxons dwelt in a Roman villa.' Almost as scarce are the instances of Saxons occupying Roman towns. Only where river, harbour or other unique geographic feature made the site irreplaceable did the newcomers continue to use it. Such a case was Greenwich, although the main part of the Roman settlement—Noviomagus—was likely to have been on the hill, with the Jutes occupying the old city, Trinovantum, on the flat plain below. The name, too, may have been changed into an imitative form with a sense recognisable to the newcomers— over some hundred of years, Anglo-Saxon armies on the continent have shown a facility for such intelligent corruption.

To his youngest daughter, Elstrudis, Alfred gave the place he called Gronovic—apparently as a marriage portion. Her husband was Baldwin II, Count of Flanders and one of the most powerful men in Europe. Alfred himself ranked as a prince of Europe, a sophisticate, a diplomat; the alliances he arranged for his children had the underlying design of furthering the cause of peace; and Baldwin, his ally (and, incidentally, son of his stepmother), had a similarly long and brave history of defiance of the Danes. Elstrudis's match was the most brilliant of the reign; we have a tiny portrait of her in the writings of her father's biographer, Bishop Asser: she was beloved by all, he said, carefully brought up, educated as befitted her rank to learn the psalms, recite English poetry and read English books—'a liberal discipline'. At her husband's court in Flanders she was loved and honoured: 'Illustrious Elstrudis, generous daughter of a King,' says her epitaph in the church of St Peter at Ghent.

Count Baldwin died in 918, and on 6 September of that year Elstrudis gave the manor of Greenwich, together with Lewisham and Woolwich, to the abbey at Ghent as a memorial to her husband, 'for the good of his soul' and that of herself and her two sons. The original charter does not exist any more, but a twelfth-century copy survives in the archives at Ghent. Again and again its contents were to be reaffirmed by English kings. In 964 Edgar, that man who styled himself 'Emperor of Britain', made an elaborate declaration of assent to the provisions, in which he described Elstrudis as 'my cousin, and daughter of the uncle of King Edward, my grandfather'. Foreign-held possessions were to prove a liability for continental foundations, and these reaffirmations were frequently necessary. Edward the Confessor, in 1016, a refugee at the court of Flanders from the Danish ravagers of England, vowed that if ever he sat on the English throne the abbey of Ghent's Greenwich possessions should be preserved to it; and two years after his accession, in 1044, he fulfilled the vow by an elaborate confirming charter.

It should perhaps be said that Elstrudis's gift did not embody full possession of the Greenwich property. What was given was manorial rights—income from such local taxes as might be imposed, certain rents, port dues, road tolls, the right to fine some classes of malefactors, and so on. It seems, too, that Alfred retained some royal possession in his Greenwich holding. For the house by the river appears to have remained in the Saxon king's hands. Although Greenwich is not mentioned in Alfred's will, its record lay perhaps in those 'booklands' which he assigned to the safe keeping of Winchester—lands protected by charter which were to remain in the possession of male heirs to the crown. And although we cannot say if any of Alfred's immediate successors occupied the place, there is the incontrovertible writ of Domesday to show that the last Anglo-Saxon king, Harold of England, held the manor here.

In one of the strangest entries in all that book, itself the most potent memorial that could have been devised to Hengist and those who followed him, the clerk wrote that in Greenwich, 'in the time of King Edward, there were two manors. Harold held one, and Brixi the other.' It is a bald title, just the name, for a king struck down defending his throne. But over the name

Harold, as a sort of conscience-stricken afterthought, the scribe has inserted Harold's Latin honour, '*Comes*' (earl).

Extract from the Domesday Book, showing the entry referring to Greenwich

1066. Harold and his Saxons stand against the Normans at the Battle of Hastings. A scene from the Bayeux Tapestry

CHAPTER 3

The Conqueror and the Flemings

It was in 1081, five years before work started on Domesday, that William the Conqueror produced his charter confirming the gifts of Elstrudis to the abbey at Ghent. The list of signatories is an impressive one, including as it does the archbishops of both Canterbury and York, nine bishops, three abbots, twenty-six of the most powerful men in Duke William's new kingdom, and two of his four sons. But what gives it its most poignant interest for Greenwich is the first name in the long list of witnesses, that of Matilda, William's wife and queen—Matilda of Flanders, great-great-great-great-granddaughter of Elstrudis herself.

This charter reflected three values: William's might and his magnanimity; the store he set on his relations with Flanders; and the importance of Greenwich. At first glance it was a backward-looking importance. As we have seen, Greenwich had begun to lessen her hold on the commercial and governmental life of the country long before the date of Elstrudis's benefaction. Perhaps, indeed, one might be cynical and say that it was only because of this decline in stature that the gift had been permitted by an astute King Alfred in the first place. One might even go further and see in this gesture an accolade, a graceful way of crowning Greenwich's long and momentous history without harming the kingdom of which it had all but ceased to be a dominating factor. Nevertheless, for both William and his queen, the signing ceremony of 1081 must have been an occasion of much private congratulation and personal happiness.

Although the important, thickly inhabited part of the manor of Greenwich must always have been that by the river, the chief Domesday entry was made under Lewisham: '*In Grenviz Hundredo.—Abbas de Gand tenet de rege, Levesham.*' The place was described as having two sulings—a suling being a peculiarly Kentish measurement roughly corresponding to the carucate or as much land as a four-yoke team of oxen could plough in a year, say on average about 160 acres. (The subsidiary manor of Charlton had one suling.) The demesne lands—that is, the lands round the mansion—had two teams, with arable land of fourteen teams. Fifty villans, or tenant farmers, together with nine bordars or cottage-holders, had seventeen teams between them. Attached to the manor were three slaves or serfs—men whose duties consisted of watching the herds, ploughing and acting as stockmen. There were eleven mills, probably most of them along the line of the Ravensbourne, and presumably for grinding corn rather than for drainage; thirty acres of meadow; and woodland sufficient to support fifty hogs. The manor revenue, which at the time of Edward the Confessor had been worth £16 per annum, had shrunk during the troubled years of conquest to £12. But by the time of the Domesday entry it had made a remarkable recovery and was worth £30, of which 'the produce of the port' amounted to 40s.

There was another side, of course, to the bequest to Ghent. However comforting it might have been to Elstrudis, and later to Matilda, to make and confirm such benefactions, to the glory of God and for the good of their souls, diplomatically speaking things were not quite so simple. Under the smile of piety, there were the bared teeth of war. Alfred himself, locked in a life and death struggle with the Danes, must have seen in this gift to his daughter's adopted land a means of securing a powerful alliance. Flanders, the most stable and progressive successor to the divided kingdom of Charlemagne, was the one continental nation that had emerged into the eleventh century as a maritime power. Very surprisingly, in view of their Viking ancestry, William's Normans seem to have lost the urge to go to sea; and had it not been for Flemish aid they could never have mounted their cross-Channel invasion. The Thames was a dagger pointing at the capital city of London; non-control of the seas meant non-control of any hand that sought to grasp it.

For Greenwich in particular, the disastrous consequences of lack of sea power were fresh in the memory. In Ethelred's day men of the abbot's manor had suffered the humiliation of having a Danish fleet anchored off their shores for several years, while a Danish army roved at will, committing unchecked depravities on the land. There had been the dreadful experience of Alfege, Archbishop of Canterbury, kidnapped from his cathedral in 1011 and brought to imprisonment in Greenwich, in a cell somewhere on the marshes, damp and infested with frogs. In spite of the terror in which his captors were held, and the knowledge that twelve of the fiercest of them guarded his prison, Alfege suffered a rescue attempt. 'Suffered' is perhaps the correct word. Someone appeared at the door of his cell at dead of night, holding a torch and quoting the scriptures. There followed a mad, Hollywood-type race, over dykes and through streams, across waterlogged fields and by soggy hedgerows, during which Alfege was unable to keep up the pace, got stuck in a bog and was recaptured by the Danes. No doubt to save his would-be rescuers, he told his captors that he had been led there by the Devil; but the explanation did not prevent their staging a trial two days later, to which he had to be brought on horseback because the fetters which he had worn round his ankles while in his cell had injured his feet and made walking impossible—a somewhat tragic marginal note to the attempt at rescue.

The Danes had hoped to get a £3,000 ransom for their captive; but Alfege forbade his impoverished followers to raise such a sum. After a council held in their hall of tented leather—which seems to have been erected at the river level rather than on the heath where tradition places the site of their encampment—a feast followed. Alfege was made a butt, first of words, then of missiles; fragments of food were hurled at him, then bones; drink, disappointment at the lack of ransom, and the archbishop's infuriating habit of quoting the scriptures at them made for a violence perhaps unintended. A particularly large bone (the skull of an ox, says tradition) felled him to the ground. A half-christianised Dane seized an axe and dispatched him. He was aged fifty-eight, the date 19 April 1012.

Even in those turbulent times the murder of an archbishop was —and was seen to be—a dreadful crime. Writing far away in Germany, the chronicler Thietmar of Merseburg reported that one of the ringleaders of the attack afterwards became crippled in his limbs, and all 'realised that he had sinned against Christ's elect'. In England, a century and a half later, another Archbishop of Canterbury was to remember. Struck down at his own altar, Thomas à Becket at the moment of death called on Alfege.

But the murder had one consequence of immediate importance. Thurkhill, leader of the Greenwich Danes, having tried in vain to dissuade them from their wicked action and having left the scene in tears, went over to Ethelred and offered him a fleet of forty-five ships, to be kept at Greenwich as a barrier against the aggressions of his compatriot, Sweyn. The protection was successful, locally at any rate, and Sweyn was obliged to switch his next attack from Kent to the Humber. But the march down England towards London conquered all before it; town after town submitted, and when it was seen that London must fall, Ethelred fled to Greenwich and took refuge on one of Thurkhill's ships, and from there sailed to the Isle of Wight and thence to Normandy.

Even after he had gone, Greenwich continued to be an unhappy focal point in the struggle for power. In 1014, the *Anglo-Saxon Chronicle* tells us, it was necessary to raise £21,000 as a payment to the Danish army lying at Greenwich; and the constant harassment from this army, camped on the high ground where, some eight and a half centuries later, Bismarck was to look down on the panoply of London and murmur: 'What a city to loot!', must have made any ordinary life for the local people impossible. In 1016, on 23 April, Ethelred died, to be succeeded by his son, Edmund Ironside. Ironside was the official choice of the councillors and citizens of London; but barely had the election ceremonies been concluded when messengers came running in to say that yet another Danish fleet was sailing up the river past Greenwich, under command of Canute.... (This was the year when Ethelred's youngest son Edward, later called the Confessor, took refuge at Ghent and made the Greenwich vow which he implemented in the charter of 1044.)

Half a century later, all these incidents must have been much in the Conqueror's mind. Because it was the key to a river defence of London, the bequest of Greenwich to Ghent must be protected, and by men powerful enough, loyal enough, and with enough interest in the maintenance of an alliance with Flanders to resist any attack. How William tried to afford this protection offers a penetrating glimpse into his Domesday method. How he tried to do it—for in spite of the exercise of great care and considerable wisdom, William the Conqueror's plans for the adherence of Greenwich to Ghent met with almost complete disaster.

The scheme, obviously, was to ring round the Ghent holding with a band of steel. So the defence of the riverside manor of Greenwich was given to Gilbert Maminot, a Norman knight of proved valour and a lifelong friend of the Conqueror. It was he who gave the funeral oration at the tragic, awful burial at Caen in 1087. In the manner of the times, and without any loss of martial power, he was in the Church. In 1066, as archdeacon of Lisieux, he had been the man who undertook the all-important mission to the Pope, to get religious backing for William's invasion of Britain. In 1072 he became Bishop of Lisieux.

Although we know that Gilbert Maminot was given, and his family held for several generations, riverside Deptford—called successively West Greenwich and Deptford Strond—it is hard to say precisely what his manor of Greenwich consisted of. The Domesday entry reads: 'In Greenwich Hundred. The Bishop of Lisieux holds, of the Bishop of Bayeux, Greenwich. It answers for two sulings. In demesne there are two teams. The arable land is . . .' Very unfortunately, the figure for arable land is lost. For it will have been noticed that so far the demesne details are identical with those of the holding of the abbot of Ghent, given under Lewisham; and there is no question that West Greenwich was part of the manor of Lewisham. The number of villans, cottars and bordars show variation; obviously, only those of Deptford have been listed. But if it could be accepted that some central duplication had taken place, if Gilbert Maminot, whose barony included the services of twenty-four knights, could be shown to have held the knights' fees of the Ghent holding— in other words, to have been directly responsible for its military defence, because the abbot was an alien—many of the obscurities of Greenwich manorial history would become clear.

Maminot was certainly a powerful man. With Sir John Fiennes he was one of the custodians of Dover Castle under Bishop Odo, Earl of Kent, that traitor half-brother of the Conqueror whose fall from grace Gilbert survived. He seems to have chosen Deptford, where there were no previous defences, for the site of his castle; Hasted suggests that its actual location may be identified with some remnants of stone foundations in the grounds of Sayes Court.

In the south of the Ghent holding was the manor of Lee, and this was given to Walter of Douai, the black-browed castellain (roughly equivalent to the French or Norman *vicomte*) of the fortress of Douai, near the border with Hainault, in what is now the Nord district of France but was then part of Flanders. Walter was known as one of the most pugnacious men in Europe, and it must have seemed a clever move to place him in support of a holding of his own mother church.

To the east of Greenwich, and also a part of the Ghent holding, lay the manor of Combe. This land was later to be divided into the triple manors of Westcombe, Middlecombe and Eastcombe, and the division used to whittle away the Flemish estates. But at the Conquest, William appears to have attached all the Combe lands to the royal manor of Dartford held by himself, and to have given possession of them to Geoffrey de Mandeville. Farther down the river, Woolwich, and Mottingham, south-west of the sheriff's manor of Eltham, were also attached in part to Dartford, and came under the protection of the Mandevilles in a similar way.

An attempt has been made to give the Mandeville family a Norman origin; but there is little doubt that Geoffrey's main connection was with the French—a very different matter in 1066 —and that he was a cadet of the great house of Senlis, whose arms he bore. The Mandeville of his estates, the name by which his grandson became so well-known in England, is likely to have been Magnavilla, or Mancaville, near Lillers, in the Pas de Calais. (His Norman origin has been assumed from an estate bearing his name at Bessin, near Barfleur; but that land was acquired through a marriage between his son Ernulf de Mandeville and Alice, daughter of Adam de Port de Bessin, who also held lands in Dartford.) A near neighbour in the Pas de Calais was Walter of Douai, whose name is on a number of eleventh-century charters concerning Magnavilla.

As Gosfridus de Magna Villa, the first Geoffrey was one of the signatories to William the Conqueror's Greenwich–Ghent charter. He was also Constable of the Tower of London and, like Walter of Douai, held stretches of the Thames on its Essex bank.

There was a second line of defence for Greenwich, an outer ring as it were, whose holders were men as powerful as the

Norman, Haimon, Sheriff of Kent, who held sixty-five acres of Woolwich and a large part of Eltham; Arnulf, Lord of Hesdin, a kinsman of the Flemish Eustace of Boulogne; and Malger, another Fleming, whose family were large benefactors to the abbey of Bourbourg, near Calais. Malger held the Crays, together with manors in Orpington, Chislehurst, Bexley and Eltham, as one of the knights of the Archbishop of Canterbury; William, son of 'Oger', who held Charlton, may well have been his son. In the event, of course, no waterborne invasion of Greenwich took place, and these men were not called upon to defend it. But almost all of them left descendants who were to play a vital part in the history of the town.

It must have seemed that the iron defences of Ghent in Greenwich had been made as impregnable as could be devised. But tragically for the Flemish men in England and for William their ally, a civil war broke out in Flanders in 1070, and William backed the losing side. The cause was a dynastic struggle for the Flemish throne between Richelde, widow of Baldwin VI, on behalf of their young son Arnulf, and Baldwin's elder brother, Robert the Frisian. At the terrible battle of Cassel, in 1071, Robert gained the victory, the Norman contingent sent to Richelde's aid by William was annihilated, and the young heir Arnulf was slain. Douai had come out on the side of Richelde. The situation must have posed a fearful dilemma for Walter and the other Flemings loyal to the countess; perhaps in that quandary lies the explanation of the fact that after William the Conqueror was dead, and as soon as his father had returned to Flanders, Robert, Walter's son, seized the Greenwich and Lewisham holdings of the abbey at Ghent, and refused to give them up. Summoned to appear before Henry I, who had reaffirmed the charter, Robert retreated to Bampton, in Devon, where the family held other manors. In his absence, Henry pronounced in favour of Ghent's right to the Greenwich holding. But there was no military power available to the abbot to dispossess the usurper, and he was forced to give Robert and his heirs a charter of tenure for a yearly £25 in rent. The document was snatched away by Robert as soon as signed, and taken to his manor at Uffculme, Devon, for safe keeping; but that house was burnt to the ground in the wars between Stephen and Matilda, and the charter consumed along with everything else. Not for more than a hundred years, until 1222, was the abbot of Ghent able to bring a second lawsuit for the return of his Greenwich property. By then all material witnesses were dead, and William Paynell, heir to the manors of Walter of Douai, had to produce two freemen, each of whom, in the legal phrase, would 'adventure themselves by combat' in any question of title.

William Paynell's two freemen, brought to the court to give witness for him—and fight, if necessary, for Greenwich—were the Greenwich man, Simon, son of Humphrey, and the Devonian, Michael. Both swore that their fathers had seen the charter and had each at the point of death made them promise to come forward and do combat with anyone who doubted the Paynell family's legal right to the land. It was an unlikely story and a thin case, and Paynell lost it—though not before he had been offered, and accepted, 101 silver marks by the prior of Lewisham, acting in Ghent's interests, to withdraw.

During his lifetime, Walter of Douai had been too powerful a man to defy; but on his death, as a mark of the royal displeasure, Henry I split his son's Devon inheritance, and half the manors were given to the heirs of Geoffrey de Mandeville. But Mandeville, too, proved an unhappy choice as a champion for Ghent. As medievalists will know, Geoffrey de Mandeville, 1st Earl of Essex, and grandson of the Conqueror's companion, became notorious throughout Europe for his treachery, as famous a turncoat as the Vicar of Bray. Supporting first Matilda and then Stephen, and screwing great rewards out of each in turn, he was so hated when he died that his body was refused burial and remained in its lead coffin, hanging on a tree in the Temple churchyard in London, 'so that it should not pollute the ground', for twenty years until the Templars relented in 1162 and gave it absolution.

It was Arnold (or Ernulf) de Mandeville, his eldest son, to whom the manor of Combe descended; and that proved not a lasting holding either. For an opposite reason—his steadfastness —Arnold met disaster. He was sent into exile by King Stephen for aiding the Empress Matilda, and the manor passed to his brother Geoffrey. Geoffrey had married Eustachia, daughter of the Count of Champagne. But the unhappy story of the Mandevilles is not complete. Eustachia conceived an aversion for Geoffrey, and refused to live with him. The king granted her a divorce and gave her, along with her manor of Combe, to a new husband, the Count of St Pol—a region in what we should now call French Flanders. Counts of St Pol held Combe, with Dartford, for some years more; but a fresh hazard was in the air. In 1185 began the wars between Flanders and France which ended with the latter's annexation of all those Flemish territories that made up Artois and the later province of Picardy. By a cruel twist, every one of William the Conqueror's Flemish champions was eventually to hold allegiance to France—a France whose relations with England were already beginning to deteriorate into what was to become the Hundred Years' War.

There remained the Maminots: Gilbert Maminot—not only the loyal, steadfast friend of the Conqueror but his compatriot. Of the energetic, virile men who helped William to the conquest of England, a surprisingly large number failed to produce male descendants after the third or fourth generation. The Maminots came into this category. Although Gilbert's grandson, Walkelin, had several sons, none seems to have survived to inherit his lands. It was to the husband of his daughter, Alice, that the Maminot barony passed—Geoffrey de Say, who gave his name to Sayes Court, Deptford, and whose mother, by one of those quirks beloved of genealogists, was Beatrix, sister of the wicked Earl of

Essex, Geoffrey de Mandeville.

The marriage between Alice Maminot and Geoffrey de Say took place in 1154, and it seems to have marked an end to the Maminot responsibility for the defence of Flemish Greenwich. In the previous generation Walkelin Maminot had given some of his Greenwich revenues to the newly founded abbey of Bermondsey, perhaps as a protest against the annexations of Walter of Douai; but Geoffrey de Say, who was Norman rather than Flemish, presumably did not feel himself involved enough to challenge the heirs of Walter for possession.

The value of Greenwich to the abbey of Ghent lay partly in actual property rentals, partly in manorial dues. These latter included tithes, quit-rents, quay dues, various fines allowed to be levied by the abbot's court, and tolls. How much of these were pressed by Walter of Douai and his heirs we have no means of telling. After 1222 and his successful lawsuit, the abbot of Ghent's accounts begin to give some picture of what the town was like. Revenue from wood thinnings, goods in kind such as farm produce, and a proportion of fruit from the local orchards, all figure in the ledgers. Apart from woods and fields, the abbey owned cottages, barns and some specialised properties such as the Paternoster Croft in Crooms Hill. There was a farm, though unfortunately we do not know where it was; it could have been at Rushey Green, Lewisham, where there was certainly a priory farmhouse in the seventeenth century. A fourteenth-century return gives a picture of its annual yield and assets: one boar, value 40s; one sow, 2s; 10 quarters of barley in sheaves, 25s; 6 ditto of rye, 30s; 3 ditto of wheat, 5s; 6 ditto of beans, 12s; one pair of wheels, newly repaired and bound with iron, 20s.

But by far the most interesting property possessed by Ghent was the house by the river, known as Old Court. This building or collection of buildings, already called old in the twelfth century, was on the site of the present Royal Naval College, perhaps a little to the eastward. If Walter of Douai made it his residence,

A drawing of the memorial window to Humphrey, Duke of Gloucester, in old St Alfege's. The church collapsed in 1710

Wenceslaus Hollar's drawing of Greenwich Castle, dated 1637

The Palace of Placentia, engraved by James Basire in 1767 from a painting belonging to Dr Ducarel

Queen Elizabeth dancing with the Earl of Leicester. The musicians on the left may be identified as Alfonso Ferrabosco, bass viol; Caesar Galliardello and Richard Farrant, treble viols; and John Lanier, sabeca

we have no record; nor do we know whether Harold of England ever stayed here during the time he held Greenwich manor. It was certainly part of the dower given to Ghent by Elstrudis, and it could well have been a residence of Saxon kings of Kent. Although the abbot held a manorial court here, that was not the start of the house's courtly function; there was a very old tradition indeed for court proceedings from this place.

The ancient British records quoted by Geoffrey of Monmouth speak of *three* Roman invasions of Britain by Julius Caesar; so does Nennius. The second closed with the fight at the Thames, where Cassivellaunus gained the victory by the placing of underwater stakes which pierced the enemy's ships. This whole incident is only obliquely glanced at by Caesar (too humiliating?), who runs it into his ultimate victory against Cassivellaunus's stronghold farther north. The inaccurate time scale may perhaps be explained by a mistranslation of a kind which has occurred elsewhere, whereby the old British word for a season has been misapplied to denote a year. According to the British account, after this second setback Caesar retreated for a time to the shores of the Morini, at Boulogne. The British thought they had won and held a joyful celebration at Trinovantum. After a sacrificial feast of gargantuan proportions, during which 40,000 cows and 100,000 sheep were slaughtered, the day ended in sport. The climax became over-rowdy; the young nephew of Cassivellaunus, a youth named Hireglas, disputed the verdict in a wrestling match with Evelinus, nephew of Androgeus; and in a sudden rage the latter snatched up a sword and cut off Hireglas's head. King Cassivellaunus ordered Evelinus to be brought to his fortress, whereupon Androgeus, suspecting the king's intentions, 'made answer that *he had a court of his own*, and that whatever should be alleged against his own men, ought to be determined there. If, therefore, he was resolved to demand justice of Evelinus, *he might have it at Trinovantum*, according to ancient custom.'

The old court by the river may well have been the place from which Hlothere, joint king of Kent with his nephew Edric, issued laws between 673 and 685. In these laws is embedded a historical mystery. One clause speaks of Hlothere's subjects repairing, when in London, to the hall of the King of Kent there. But possession of London in those years was held not by Kent but by the East Saxons. Although he may not have been aware of it, Hlothere's London hall is likely to have had a much older title than any Saxon one. It was almost certainly situated on the ground called Waremansacre, which the charter of Edward the Confessor was to include with Elstrudis's gift to Ghent. This ground was at the eastern extremity of the city of London, running down river along what is now Tower Ward. It had a wharf, stalls, and the valuable right to hold a market, and its western end abutted on the dock at Billingsgate.

What was the link that joined so persistently the Billingsgates of Greenwich and London? Is there a clue in the strange, indeed inexplicable, tradition whereby medieval porters at the London fishmarket had a custom—which they themselves did not pretend to understand—whereby a newcomer to the wharf was asked to choose one of themselves for a godfather, pay sixpence and genuflect to an old post, or be bumped on it. It was, they said, a kind of christening; something to do with a change of name.

All over the world, tolls or customs are an extremely ancient practice. References to London port dues occur as early as 734, though they must, of course, have been instituted much earlier. Before the first London custom house of which we have record was built, these dues were paid at or near the wharf at Billingsgate—or rather, the wharf at Waremansacre which adjoined it. Although Edward the Confessor's Ghent charter is the first to make specific mention of Waremansacre, subsequent documents speak of it as 'belonging to Greeenwich', and there is little doubt that it was because of an already existing Greenwich ownership that Elstrudis included it in her original gift. But how could it have come about that the people of Greenwich owned this vital point, seat of the port dues, at the very entrance to the city of London?

One translation of the name Waremansacre equates it with 'warrior's acre'—the ground of the soldiers. There are, of course, legends going back to Roman times linking the site of the Tower with a military fortress; they are mostly denied by historians. But Greenwich's possession of Waremansacre is fact.

Suppose one were to go back to the middle of the first century BC when Greenwich was being threatened by Roman invasion, and London did not exist—to that quarrel between the inhabitants of the capital city of Trinovantum and the would-be founders of a safer place upstream? Could it be that in the Waremansacre ownership we are glimpsing the vestiges of a commercial arrangement whereby hard-headed statesmen of the older place saw their port being by-passed, and made an agreement whereby peaceful passage and undisturbed docking facilities would be permitted higher up the river only on condition that the customs due to Trinovantum were still allowed to accrue to it? Antiquarians disagree as to the derivation of the name London. Geoffrey of Monmouth's stab at 'Lud's town' never did find much support among etymologists. But *lhong* is the ancient British word for ship; there is an associated word, now obsolete, in Gaelic, which is *lonquhard*, meaning a temporary dwelling or hut. What handier instant accommodation to a primitive man pushing his way up river than an upturned boat? And some of the Roman earliest accounts of London give it the name Longinium, or Longhinium.

Thirteenth-century records of Greenwich show many men of Flemish origin among its citizens. Names of tenants include Pychard and Picard, Loos, Flemmyng and Le Flameng, Astyng, Walkelin and Le Doo—the last probably an approximation for Douai. The fiery Walter had no doubt found homes for his followers here. The tragedy was that after 1187 these men were drawn to a loyalty with France, not Flanders; and it becomes more and more plain from the rolls that they resented any impositions rated by Ghent.

The unfortunate abbot, whose first few years of repossession had been devoted to repairing his property, now when he started to enforce the dues that justified such outlay found himself hopelessly at odds with the town. On one day a year, wool-carts crossing the king's highway to the quay were mulcted of a toll of $1\frac{1}{2}$d each; but so unacceptable had this impost become by 1298 that a charge of highway robbery was laid against the abbot. So much for the honeyed words of King John in his charter of 1209 to the monks of Ghent—idle as well as too sweet, since those were the days when Walter's descendants still held the place. Nevertheless, he ordered:

> Let them be free of court decrees, complaints, shires and hundreds, in the borough and out of it; and from geld, lot and scot, on and off the water, in pastures and out of them, and on the plains, as fully, freely and honourably as ever they held them in the times of King Edward, King William, my grandfather King Henry, and of my father. We also wish them to have the water courses to conduct them where they please; and that they may have their fisheries, pools, lakes and wild fowl below the circuit of the town; and that they may have our security as to their mills which are on their lands, as to their thelonium, and as to their measures of provisions and beer...

By 1275 the local discontent was loud enough to reach the public ear of the king and cause him to order an investigation into the muniments of the priory of Lewisham which comprised and dealt with the Greenwich holding. The abbot of Ghent was summoned from Flanders; he seems to have managed to put some of his difficulties before Edward I, for the king gave him permission to sell Lewisham to the bishop of Rochester—although it is virtually certain that he did not do so. A review of taxation in 1291 revealed that the Greenwich and Lewisham income of the abbey amounted to some £70 a year, while the London holding (presumably Waremansacre) brought in 16s 10d. In 1299 the abbot was fined £40 for taking the yearly highway toll without a warrant; and although he was eventually able to obtain a pardon for this offence, it must have become apparent to everybody that Elstrudis's gift no longer had the cooperation of the citizens of Greenwich without whose support it could not be sustained. Already in 1295 somebody had pointed out that the number of foreigners in the district constituted a danger to the realm on account of the strategic importance of the river Thames. And by 1337, and the start of the Hundred Years' War with France, Edward III had been persuaded to take the abbey's possessions into his own hands, ostensibly for the national safety. The 1414 Bill of Henry V, whereby the possessions of alien monasteries were disallowed, was, in Greenwich at any rate, no more than a climax to a long stretch of Flemish disappointment.

One can see how the king's not unwilling hand was forced. Complaints about the national danger; complaints that the abbey was neglecting its duty of maintaining four chantries a day for the souls of the founders; complaints that the distribution of alms, laid down in the articles for each Thursday and Friday, had lapsed—though what alms the abbot was supposed to distribute when he was debarred from collecting dues was not suggested—all these added up to an untenable position for Ghent. So the bequest of 'the generous daughter of an English king' for the safety of her family's souls for ever was finally quashed. By the time Henry V's Statute of 1414 came to be passed, it had lasted just four short of five hundred years. Perhaps Elstrudis should have been grateful that a mortal's 'for ever' had endured so long.

CHAPTER 4

'*La Maison de Grenewic*'

The focal point of Greenwich must always have been the great house by the river; and it would be of enormous interest to local historians to find out what it was like. In the absence of real evidence, we can only guess. A lucid and scholarly book, *The English Medieval House*, by Margaret Wood (Mrs E. G. Kaines-Thomas), goes into the question of the social and domestic attitudes that made for the form of Norman manor houses. With few exceptions these were based on the great hall, with a solar, or private family apartment, built at one end at first-floor level and reached by an external spiral staircase. Because of the risk of fire, kitchens and cooking houses were separate structures.

But the great house at Greenwich was not Norman; nor is it likely to have been Flemish. Indeed, inherent in the confirmatory charters of Saxon kings is also the confirmation that it was there in Elstrudis's day; the twelfth-century description of it as the 'old house' is appropriate to a building put up before 918. We do not know where the palace of Androgeus, Duke of Trinovantum, was—though there is no reason to suppose that he would have been satisfied with a less good site than those who followed him. Nor do we know what his house would have been like. But for an imaginative reconstruction of the building of his successors, we might look where they exist at descriptions of the royal residences of Anglo-Saxon kings. One of these, the palace of the kings of Northumbria, at Yeavering, Northumberland, where Ethelburga of Kent went to be queen in 627, has lately been excavated. The archaeologist in charge, Brian Hope-Taylor, described it as having a great hall with porches, and a complex, linked but separate, of large and small structures round it, one of which was a pagan temple later adapted to Christian worship. These buildings were of wood, heavily buttressed.

The palace of the kings of Wessex, at Cheddar, Somerset, was also of wood. The great hall was about 80ft long by 18ft wide, its walls being curved so that the middle section was broader. Possibly this hall, and certainly the West Saxon hall at Calne, Wiltshire, had an upstairs room, since we know that the floor of the latter collapsed in 978 during a meeting of the Witan. Beowulf's description of Heorot, the royal hall of Hrothgar, king of the Danes, indicates considerable richness; in the words of Margaret Wood, 'the impression given is that of a highly ornamental barn.' John R. Clark Hall, who produced a study of *Beowulf* in 1901, wrote: 'Think of Heorot and its surroundings. There is a throne, tapestry on the wall, gold adornments, iron bars to the door, a mead-plain, bowers, a paved way. There is wine at the feasts—not merely ale and mead. There is much reference to the goldsmith's art—men and women wear costly jewellery of cunning workmanship. The men are fighters—rough and forceful; it is to the women that refinement and diplomacy belong.' One might almost be re-reading Geoffrey of Monmouth's description of the court of Vortigern.

The Greenwich house is likely to have reflected the wooden Anglo-Saxon pattern, one known to be traceable to prehistoric times and to Friesland, where Hengist and Horsa came from. It might not be too fanciful to suggest that some embellishment, such as paving for the courts, could have been introduced with stone robbed from the Roman buildings up the hill. Nor in this context should we forget the tessellated pavement found under the site of the Greenwich power station, eastward of the present Royal Naval College. The succession of Greenwich palaces seems always to have been renewed to the west, possibly owing to the gradual build-up on its western side of the river loop which had already formed the spit of land now known as the Isle of Dogs— an almost imperceptibly changing glance in the eye of that miraculous view along two reaches of the Thames.

The thirteenth-century accounts of the abbot of Ghent show that the house in his day was not only still habitable but perhaps even still magnificent. As well as the premises used for his court (perhaps the great hall, certainly some ancillary offices), there was accommodation in a 'hostel' big enough, and grand enough, for the entertainment of visiting prelates. The conduits under the park, already discussed, brought that great luxury, running water, to the rooms. And a ledger of 1271 lists among other outgoings the provision of food and wine, servants' clothes and their wages, embroideries and linen. These were the great days of the *Opus Anglicanum* so the embroideries, some of which were vestments, would almost certainly have originated in England. But the linen came from Flanders. As early as 1099, Robert II, Count of Flanders, far away in the Holy Land on the triumphant first crusade, had declined the crown of Jerusalem with the words: 'I promised the Countess my wife to return to her on fulfilling my vow. It is very long since I could take a hot or a cold bath, or sleep between white sheets. And it is well known how accustomed are the Flemings to comfortable beds and well warmed houses.'

No doubt this Flemish comfort was appreciated by the stream of abbots and priors who, the accounts show, were visitors to the Greenwich house. A note of 1326 mentions a stay by the prior of Salisbury, and specifies a charge of $4\frac{1}{2}$d for three days' fodder for his horse. But at some time early in the fourteenth century the abbot let his domestic buildings, or some of them, only holding back accommodation for his courts. It was the first real loosening of the Flemish hold, the first non-private acknowledgement of failure. After what must have been an agonising appraisal of the situation, the abbot chose as tenant a Rokesley.

The Rokesleys were a well known Kent family whose most famous member was that Gregory de Rokesley, eight times mayor of London, who refused to sink his mayoral authority under the king's justiciars and was imprisoned for the defiance. That was in 1285. But earlier, Gregory had been called in to advise on financial matters, and was put in charge of the mint. He was also made consultant to the king on affairs connected with Flanders. Although he was a goldsmith by craft (and famous as the richest of them) his chief interest was the wool trade. By the end of the thirteenth century some 6,000 lengths of Flemish cloth were being brought up the Thames to London each year, and Rokesley's business, or part of it, consisted in shipping out the English wool that was the raw material.

But the most fascinating thing about Gregory de Rokesley is his ancestry. For in this man was embodied the last defensive strand of the rope woven by William the Conqueror for the protection of the Ghent properties in Greenwich. Gregory was the direct heir and descendant of Malger, the Flemish knight who had been given Domesday manors in that outer ring of Greenwich defence comprising Foot's Cray, Paul's Cray, North Cray, Bexley, Chislehurst, Eltham and the Ruxley district of Orpington; this last place eventually gave its name to the family.

It is obvious that Malger must have retained his links with his homeland; unlike so many of the Domesday tenants, he was not content just to be soldier and landlord. He went into commerce; he must, indeed, have a claim to be the first commuter. The twelfth-century disasters that overtook Flanders were later to force many a Flemish lord's son to turn to trade; Malger was on the scene early, and by choosing to become shipowner and merchant of the city of London he also illustrates for us, at least in part, how that city's wealth and influence were created. Not everyone of the companions of the Conqueror remained an aristocrat.

No doubt it was a gradual transition; Gregory's great-grandfather had gone to the Crusades with Richard I; but by his own lifetime the country gentleman was almost wholly replaced by the city merchant. Nor did the king find a Rokesley purse less valuable than a Rokesley sword. Although it is difficult to be specific about it, Edward I's constant recourse to Gregory for advice, the latter's appointment as master of the exchange, the special mission by which he and Henry Waleys took 6,000 marks to the king in Wales—all these acts point to an intimate royal relationship concerned with money. The king's wars were expensive—that was not new. But an arrangement with merchants of the city of London by which he might privately, perhaps even secretly, be financed was.

It has long been a matter of uncertainty how the royal family regained for themselves possession of Greenwich. William the Conqueror (perhaps because of its links with Harold) had been happy to assign everything to Flanders. For his successors possibly the quarrel with Walter of Douai and the Paynells had made a royal presence in the manor too embarrassing. As we have seen, the Ghent accounts show that the abbot was concerned to keep a firm hold on the riverside house. Yet there are persistent threads in a cord that would bind the Edwards and Henry IV to Greenwich.

Is it possible that one of these threads came through the Rokesleys? Confusion has been caused because another royal house was built in the manor of Greenwich, that at Redriffe (Rotherhithe), on the extreme western boundary of the manor. Hasted attributes the building of that house to King John, whose death in 1216 occurred six years before Ghent regained possession from the Paynells in 1222. Attempts have been made to explain that Edward I, who gave Lenten offerings to the chapel of the blessed Mary at Greenwich in 1300, and Edward III, who often resided 'at Greenwich', in fact always stayed at the house in Rotherhithe. Henry IV, whose will was dated from his manor of Greenwich on 21 January 1408, is also thought by many historians to have written it from Rotherhithe, 'because the East Greenwich manor was held by the abbot of Ghent'. But the facts do not sustain this supposition.

We do not know when the first Rokesley lease was negotiated, but it was almost certainly in Gregory de Rokesley's lifetime. Gregory died in 1291. Both his sons were knighted by Edward I; the younger, Sir Richard, was made governor of Montreuil. (Was it a last clutch by the family at their chivalric origins—or an acknowledgement by the king that he owed a private debt?) Neither knight apparently left sons, and Gregory's Kent possessions were inherited by his nephew, Roger, son of his sister Agnes. This Roger in 1305 settled at least some of his manors on John Abel of Sydenham and his wife Margaret; and, possibly by mistake, property held by the abbot of Ghent and leased to the Rokesleys was included in the transfer. (Or was there some sinister dealing, revealed in the fact that a John Abel, prior of Lewisham in 1298, had later to be removed for an unstated misdemeanour?)

The error, if such it was, was compounded in 1314, when Roger's son, also Roger, repeated the transaction to the Abels, conveying to them all his rights in his manors of 'Fotescray, Chiselhurst, Paulscray, Bexley, Northcray, Eltham and Rokesle'. Although the Greenwich holdings were again not specified, jurors in a lawsuit of 1322, one of them Gregory de Rokesley, grandson (or more probably grand-nephew) of the late mayor, found that John Abel had died seized of 'the manor of Lewisham [ie Greenwich] worth 100s clear, with the water mill at Deptford, also worth 100s clear, held of the abbot of Ghent'. The Ghent holdings had plainly been acquired by the Abels illegally, and in 1343, as Hasted correctly reports, they escheated to the crown. His editors considered that Hasted must have made a mistake, since these were holdings of an alien priory and could not escheat before the suppression act of 1414; but they seem to have been content to leave unprobed the manifest confusions that had now

crept into the situation. And we can note that the sum of 200s
quoted above exactly equals the £10 given as the amount of rent
paid by the king to Ghent when he took the manor into his pro-
tective custody in time of war.

There seems about this time to have sprung up a real cleavage
between the actions of Ghent and those of the crown. In this
same year, 1343, a lease of the manor 'et des biens qui en
dependant' was granted by the abbot of Ghent to William Predhomme. Gosselyn Rym and Eustace Ghentbrugge, described as
the abbot's proctors, conducted the negotiations; many more
rights, perhaps more possessions, must have been included, because the rent was to be £50 per annum, the term twenty years.
But within about eighteen months this lease seems, at least at the
English end, to have been cancelled. Predhomme is a very
French-sounding name, and this was a time when Edward III
was being petitioned about the prevalence in the vicinity of the
Thames of foreign spies. By 1347 both the manor and the Deptford mill had been re–assigned to John de Rokesley, Roger's
heir. But whether all these gyrations of the law were cloaking
an arrangement between the Rokesleys and the king by which
the latter was able to enjoy the Greenwich mansion I have not
been able to confirm. It seems at least likely, and the likelihood
is reinforced by such a clue as the debt of £100 acknowledged
by William Sergotz, the abbot's proctor, as being due in 1343
to John de Rokesley, the cause unspecified. Could it have been
two years' rent, illegitimately received from Predhomme? There
is also the anomaly that the 1347 lease was drawn up between
Ghent and Rokesley at a time when Edward III was known to
be in possession of the manor, ostensibly because of the wars
with France. But 'the manor of Lewisham', that is, Greenwich,
and parcels of land actually in Lewisham are inextricably mixed
up in the old documents; and one can be sure only that as time
went on, not only was the 'ferme'—the right to take revenue—
sub-leased, but more and more of the abbot's actual properties

were also let off, to a diversity of tenants some of whom paid to the prior of Lewisham, others to the king.

Certainly we are now entering a period during which the kings of England wanted, some of them quite passionately, the return of the manor of Greenwich to the physical possession of the crown. For diplomatic reasons there could, of course, be no question of an out-and-out seizure, and the legal barriers were both cumbersome and enduring. With the benefit of hindsight it is easy to observe the slowly mounting pressure; yet, individual royal acts concerned with the manor's return were surprisingly restrained. No reign made one single step forward which could truly be called decisive; no monarch by his sole individual action determined the outcome. As it referred to Greenwich, at any rate, Henry V's Act of 1414 simply translated an unendurable situation into an acceptable one—emotion being served rather than justice. We are left with the fascinating question of how much each king was the tool of an extraneous, even mysterious, force; how much each man assessed and then slotted his own deeds into a framework which was to encompass far more than his own lifetime. Everything about Greenwich betokens not only a long history but a gigantic time scale, as if the place itself had a life and a will of its own. In this context, and before he vanishes from these pages, it is worth pointing out that John de Rokesley's other Kentish manor was Lullingstone—that Lullingstone which, with Plumstead and half of Greenwich (the other half belonging to Harold, King of England), had been held before the Conquest by Brixi Celt. As John de Rokesley was the last of William's champions elected to serve the court of the abbot of Ghent, so, in this long history of Greenwich, his family's predecessor, the British Brixi, might well have been the last heir of the court of Androgeus, Duke of Trinovantum.

At Christmas, 1366, Christo Cosimo, prior of Lewisham, obtained the king's licence to visit Flanders, and to take with him one bow, twenty arrows, one pipe of salted beef, eight bacons and three barrels of beer for the sustenance of himself and two attendants on the journey. There is no hint anywhere that he returned or was replaced. Indeed, all the evidence shows that from this time on the administration of Greenwich was conducted from Ghent by the abbot himself.

The prior's departure must have resulted in considerable confusion, one effect of which has been the misunderstanding by later historians of the ecclesiastical difficulty caused. Without the controlling hand of the prior of Lewisham there would be no one to conduct services—something unthinkable in the Middle Ages. Whoever had the right of it, *de facto* possession was now with the crown, and the medieval conscience would demand nothing less than that Edward III should make provision for some sort of religious observance. So he did, establishing a monastery of friars minorites. The date is given as 1376, when he was ill, in fact dying; both John Speed, writing in 1611, and John Weever make categoric references to it. Unfortunately, the editors of Hasted, who found themselves unable to acknowledge the existence of this foundation, are nowadays taken as the authority; but, not having followed the slow retreat of the abbot, they failed to understand the nature of the gap created by Cosimo's withdrawal; presuming that Ghent was still in possession, they inferred that Speed and Weever must of necessity be mistaken. But the references are too precise to be dismissed; and the need itself must be the corroboration.

On 22 June 1377 Edward died at Shene, and was succeeded by his grandson, Richard II. For a short time Greenwich's fate was in the hands of a king who preferred Eltham. It was a disastrous phase for the town, with neither abbey nor crown in command. Eventually the 'waste and delapidation' became so great that Richard was at last forced to institute an inquiry into its cause. The reason was not far to seek; Rokesley's lease must have lapsed soon after the departure of Cosimo; and charge of the manor had been awarded to that rebel-slayer, Alderman

Nicholas Brember, a London grocer, knighted, like William Walworth, at the scene of Wat Tyler's death in 1381. There was also a nominee of Ghent, Henry Vannere, to whom with other citizens of London the abbot had offered a twenty-year lease in 1376. Vannere's stewardship could not have been all that bad, since Ghent expressed itself happy with the measures he had adopted for flood prevention. But Brember milked Greenwich without maintaining it; and he allowed the 'court bridge' or pier next to the palace to fall down, so that the trade of the place was severely handicapped. This corrupt man met a picturesque end, being executed with, according to Holinshed, 'an axe of his own design'; and, as understood in England at any rate, custodianship of the Ghent holdings at Greenwich was given to the king's treasurer, John Norbury.

Norbury himself was a not unpicturesque character. A young soldier adventurer, he had fought for Portugal in the wars with Castile, and in 1390 he accompanied the future Henry IV on the latter's expedition to Prussia; throughout his life he was in close attendance on Henry, who was accustomed to refer to him as 'our dear squire'. Royal household accounts reveal that he lent the king money—as much as £2,000 in 1407 and another £2,000 two years later. Like Rokesley, he had a connection with the wool trade which may have brought him personal links with Greenwich; his first wife, Petronella Stoday, had a rich Greenwich father, Sir Richard Stoday, himself a one-time tenant of Ghent. Norbury must have spent time and money restoring the abbot's property at Greenwich; it was without doubt he who was behind Edward III's friars minorites here. 'John Norbury,' writes John Weever in 1631, 'founded a priory in this town of Lewisham, which he replenished with black monk aliens, belonging to the abbey of Ghent in Flanders.' And again, under Greenwich, Weever writes: 'Here in this town was another monastery of fryars minorites and aliens, founded by King Edward III and the foresaid John Norbury, which, as Lewisham did, belonged to the abbot of Ghent in Flanders.'

It was from his manor of Greenwich, refurbished by his squire, that Henry IV on 21 January 1408 dated a hastily drawn-up will. He had been brought from Eltham, in what was believed to be a dying condition, in the hope that the Greenwich air might revive him. 'The will,' says James Hamilton Wylie, Henry IV's biographer, 'forms a marked contrast to those of any previous kings, and seems to bear the stamp of panic.' Contrary to custom, it was written in 'good, modern English', and after the usual plea for forgiveness for a misspent life, and a request that he should be buried at Canterbury, he left instructions that 'all his debts are to be quit; fees, gifts and wages paid; six of his personal servants to be rewarded for their services by his son; and the queen's dowry to be charged on the revenues of the Duchy of Lancaster.' Greenwich was not mentioned; but nor was any other property of the king's. 'As it turned out,' comments Wylie, 'the goods would not stretch to pay ordinary debts, so that it was perhaps wise to abstain from gifts based upon an imaginary surplus.'

The pure Thames air (and possibly the drainage system, flushed twice daily by the tide) seems to have done the trick, and Henry recovered. Later, he fulfilled a wish that Norbury should continue in possession of Greenwich; by a deed dated 1412, when he was again dreadfully ill and within a few months of his actual death, his 'dear squire' was granted for life, 'of the king's special grace and own motion, and not at his insistence or supplication, and for a certain sum of money paid at the receipt of the king's chamber . . .' all that the abbot of Ghent had once enjoyed.

Nineteenth-century attempts to equate all Henry's visits to Greenwich with sojourns at the Rotherhithe house built by King John do not survive examination. The household accounts of the reign show that a clear distinction is made between Rotherhithe (where, for instance, he stayed in May 1411, 'whiles,' said Lambarde, 'he was cured of a Leprosie') and his manor of Green-which. A number of documents issued from Rotherhithe are specifically so headed; and wardrobe accounts differentiate between fees to boatmen paid for ferrying to Rotherhithe and to Greenwich. There is no reason to doubt that he occupied both; the fifteenth-century scale of distances would have made them as separate from each other as either was from Eltham.

John Norbury died leaving a second wife, Elizabeth Botiller, sister of Lord Sudeley. She had herself been married before, to that Sir William Heron whose own first wife was the last of the Deptford Says. For her third husband, Elizabeth Norbury took the courtier Sir John Montgomery. He set about selling her late husband's possessions, seeming to have forgotten that Norbury's Greenwich holding was for his lifetime only. Or was this merely the last irresistible culmination in the spiral of royal possession? For in 1426 Montgomery sold Norbury's lease of the estates of the abbey of Ghent to Thomas Beaufort, Duke of Exeter. Beaufort had been present at the death-bed of his nephew, Henry V, in France, and had there been appointed guardian of the king's infant son; according to Dugdale, it was at Henry's wish that he acquired Greenwich. Whether that was true or not, the official transfer of the property came, for him, only just in time. Dating his will, like Henry IV whose half-brother he was, from his manor of Greenwich on 29 December 1426, before the year was done, Beaufort was dead. His guardianship of the infant Henry VI and his possession of the manor of Greenwich both passed to Henry V's youngest brother, Humphrey, Duke of Gloucester.

Before the abbot and Ghent are quite forgotten, and long before any plans by Humphrey could have been formulated for a great new house by the river, there appears a faint, evocative description of the old one.

It was towards the end of the fourteenth century—when no doubt an echo had reached Flanders of the masses being sung at Greenwich, to the glory of the God both countries worshipped but in the name of Edward rather than St Peter of Ghent, when

Henry Vannere's lease was at last running out and some desperate attempt must be made now, if at all, to reassert rights—that the abbot decided to obtain first-hand information about his properties. On 9 June 1396 an agent called Gille Delaporte was sent from Flanders for the purpose of making a private assessment of the Greenwich holding. His report, dated 30 June of that year, is still at Ghent. Much of the property, which he seems to have examined thoroughly if furtively, was dilapidated, though most was let. There was a long question-and-answer section in the report, dealing with the destination of various revenues which had plainly not been reaching Ghent. To all questions concerning the tenant-in-chief—'Does Henry Vannere hold all these goods or does the king?'—the answer came sad but clear: *On dit que le Roy les a tous.'* Of the great house by the river, Delaporte wrote:

La maison de Grenewyc siet sur la rivière Thamise et est la première maison de la ville de Grenewic en venant de Flandres. Si est ledit hostel bien retenus, une porte couverte de tieulles vers les champs et toutes les autres maisons couvertes destrain et ny demeure personne que ung concièrge que on appelle Henry Brioul et n'a cun oel.

The river approach to Greenwich in the 17th century

CHAPTER 5

Duke Humphrey's Bella Court

From his mother, Mary de Bohun, Humphrey, Duke of Gloucester, drew into his veins the blood of Maminot, Mandeville and Say. Through the King of England, his father, there was a descent from the pre-Conquest Athelings, Alfred the Great, and the kings of Wessex and Kent. His grandfather had been born in Ghent and he himself was briefly to hold the title of Count of Flanders. Through the Conqueror's consort, Matilda, Elstrudis herself was his ancestress. No man in England could have had closer bonds with the ancient territorial traditions of Greenwich. But Humphrey was a forward-looking man, a modernist, and the house he started to put up about 1430 was as new as he could make it.

For all the religious shuffling of the preceding hundred years, there was still an ecclesiastical hold on the manor of Greenwich, and negotiations had to be completed with the newly–founded priory of Shene, to which Henry V had made over the rights of Ghent, before he could build. The first stage was to arrange with Shene to acquire a title to seventeen acres of 'pasture and some rough land' which had belonged to Ghent. There were also licences to be obtained under the Privy Seal. These speak of permission to 'enclose and empark 200 acres of land [including that obtained from Shene], pasture, wood, heath, furze and gorse', to be held to the duke and his heirs for ever. Other licences allowed him to 'build a mansion, crennelled and embattled, and enclose it within walls, also to erect and turrelate a certain tower, all in stone and lime, within the park'. The licences range from 1432 to 1436, and some of them contain the words *de novo*. They make it obvious that Humphrey's work was a rebuilding, both of the tower and of the house by the river; and that he must have occupied the old abbey mansion for several years before the new palace was completed. The official report of the 1970–71 archaeological dig is not yet published; but it is known that substantial earlier remains of a chalk or stone building were uncovered, right against the east wall of Humphrey's Bella Court.

What emerges from this discovery, coupled with a study of the documents—and it is apparent both from Humphrey's occupancy of the old apartments and from the wording of Gille Delaporte's report—is that his new house was built within the same group, only slightly to the westward, and that the universal impression given by nineteenth-century writers that the complex of Old Court was totally outside Humphrey's boundary to the east can no longer be sustained. One key to the old plan lies in its gatehouses, which must have given on to roads. Gille Delaporte's description runs: 'Here is the said *hostel* well maintained, a gatehouse covered with tiles towards the fields.' Many French dictionaries still give the word *hostel* its old meaning of 'king's palace'. And the gatehouse that looked on to fields must, surely, have been the one on the Roman road which ran diagonally across the park and under the south-west corner of the Queen's House, as described by J. E. G. de Montmorency and quoted in Chapter 1. Although by forming Maze Hill Humphrey converted the diagonal road into a rectangular one, this gatehouse remained, later to be replaced by the House of Delight built for his queen by James I and VI. Either it or a two-storey, two-gabled successor may be seen in Wyngaerde's drawings of 1558, and his picture shows it at the angle it must have had to sit on the Roman road.

There would, of course, have been other gatehouses, one east, one west. The latter would have been by the landing stage, the 'bridge' as it was called in medieval times, and on the north-south roadway which was the predecessor of the Friars' Road. The former must have been near the collection of abbey buildings which Humphrey left outside his wall eastward, where ecclesiastical business was no doubt still carried on until the 1530s, and which he would not have wanted intruding upon his private domain. This must have given on to the old road to Woolwich.

It should not be forgotten that all Greenwich was the original manor of Old Court. But after Humphrey's carving out and walling or fencing his manor of Bella Court, later Plesaunce, and later still the Tudor Placentia, the remaining eastward fragment of the abbot's buildings, and the other scattered possessions east and west of Plesaunce not taken by the crown, constituted the manorial estate under the name of Old Court which later passed to Sir John Morden and is still the property of Morden College. This partitioning was not properly understood by Edward Hasted, and later historians failed to explain away his confusion.

It may be wondered why Humphrey took no more for his park, why he should not have moved his boundary eastward to bring in Westcombe. In fact, this was seen by some local men as a sensible thing to do, and of the three divisions into which the manor of Combe had now fallen, Westcombe and Spitelcombe (or Middlecombe) were offered to Edward IV in 1465 by the then holder, Thomas Ballard. The offer was rejected, no doubt for the same reasons that had motivated the Duke of Gloucester. If Humphrey had brought Westcombe within his fence, the old road could have run across the top of his park (as of course the Charlton Way does now), to join Crooms Hill, and the new track down Maze Hill would not have had to be made. But had he done this, the still remaining administrative buildings of Old Court, by now in the possession of the priory of Shene, would have been cut off, with all clerical business done there of necessity passing across his land. More serious, there would then have been no direct road communication between the old town of Greenwich and its equally old easterly neighbour, Woolwich, with a consequent great increase of people using the right of way in front of the palace, along the river bank. That there was an ancient right of way here is proved by the fact that when Christopher Wren was designing his Thames-side façade, the closed balustrading he had prepared had to be scrapped, so that the 'five-foot walk' conceded as a right of the people of Greenwich should be retained. Similarly, the great tower of the Tudor palace, which stuck out so that it had its base in the water, had to have east and west doorways cut in it, to allow this free public passage along the river bank.

Humphrey's enclosure of his estate enables us to examine the condition of Greenwich as it was in the 1430s. As has been said, his most important action was to divert the Roman road running through the park. He had to obtain a licence to do this, and to undertake to replace the closed highway with an equally useful one of the same length for the town's inhabitants. This resulted in the formation of Maze Hill. So far as we know, there were no early houses in it, although an inn, at one stage called the Crown, can later be found just below the point where the Roman road ran under the park fence; the site is nos 111–15 Maze Hill.

On the west, Humphrey took his boundary line to the existing road down Crooms Hill. This ancient way must have known the footsteps of the Danish murderers of St Alfege as they walked from their camp on Blackheath to the Danish fleet anchored in the river; older footsteps also sounded on it, belonging to Hengist's court, Vortigern's, and the ducal palace of Androgeus. This was the natural way from the Blackheath heights to the river, and all men who moved about in these parts must at one time or another have used it. It is documented from 918; one of Elstrudis's gifts to the abbey of Ghent is specifically mentioned as being in Crooms Hill—the venerable Paternoster Croft, house, barn and four acres of ground, still today there recognisable as the Grange, although naturally a thousand years of changing ownerships have wrought some differences. Then, too, this must have been one of the ways to the great cave hollowed out of the chalk, according to that primitive legend wherein Estrildis the beautiful was kept for seven years by King Locrin and bore to him a daughter named Sabrina—drowned in the Severn, as all poets of the antique know. There is an interesting corroboration for the royal ownership of this cave; Ghent documents of 1281 indicate that it was specifically included in the original manorial gift of Elstrudis.

We know St Alfege's church was there from the eleventh century, built by a shocked community on the very ground where their murdered archbishop had been struck down. It had a square tower at the west end, with what seems to have been a shingled spire rising out of it, and the nave had north and south side aisles. There was a large porch to the north, and a door at the east end of the south side, which gave on to the street; this was Church Street, running down towards Billingsgate and the river, and following almost exactly the line it takes today. The only medieval houses in this ancient street which have survived at all into the twentieth century are in the group nos 15 to 21, their shop fronts brought up to date in successive centuries, and most of the characteristics one would expect to see in such early buildings modernised away. But the narrow façades and the tall pitch of the roofs give a small peep into what Humphrey's Greenwich must have looked like. Gille Delaporte's reference to tiled roofs suggests that up to the fourteenth century town buildings not in the abbot's complex may have been of thatch. This was so prevalent a roofing material, and such a fire danger, that in many towns by about 1310 widespread instructions were being given to replace it as a building material with tiles or shingles.

There was also a market. The Waremansacre privileges, their origin long since forgotten, must gradually have come to be resented by citizens of London who saw no reason for them; one by one, other wharves had been built upstream of the Greenwich holding by the Tower, collecting other dues; and in a charter of Henry I the market, which had been there since before men could remember, was tactfully removed to the borough: 'They are to hold their market place in Gronevic, and the traders of that ville are to enjoy the King's peace going to and returning from London...' Presumably no one recalled Trinovantum and no one, so far as we know, protested. But as late as 1336, when the shadow of the forthcoming wars between France and England made the abbot of Ghent take steps to protect himself, among an inventory of his titles and other old documents lodged for safe keeping with the friars minorites in London we find the entry: '*Scripta de concordia facta cum Custode pontis Londiniensis, quodque scripta et III habent.*'

Although fifteenth-century Greenwich was compact by present-day standards, it was not insubstantial, and Hasted's description of it as a 'small fishing town' is considerably less than the truth. Gregory de Rokesley was only one of the earliest named of a very long line of rich London merchants who had marine business here, as well as comfortable, semi-rural homes. Drake's *Hundred of Blackheath* lists nearly a hundred property transactions of the thirteenth and fourteenth centuries, most of them expensive and luxurious. (Such terms are, of course, used in relation to their times; one century's grand house or great city can be the near-slum of another.) But although there must have been some hovels, some poverty, these early contracts exchanged tell of messuages, tofts, gardens, orchards and meadows, and transmit to us a whiff of elegance and cultivated space. We have a poet's description of fourteenth-century life in Greenwich:

> When passed was almost the month of May,
> And I had roamed, all the summer's day
> The grene meadow . . .
> Home to mine house full swiftly I me sped;
> And, in a little arbour that I have,
> Y-benched new with turves fresh y-grave,

I bade men should me my couch make;
For dainty of the new summer's sake,
I bade them strew flowers on my bed ...
I fell on sleep within an hour or two;
Me mette how I lay in the meadow tho,
To see this flower that I so love and dread ...

Geoffrey Chaucer, writing a poem about a daisy; prophetic Chaucer, who almost certainly lived in Greenwich between 1385 and 1399, and in between the intervals of sitting on the king's commission for walls and ditches (an honour which he shared with Henry Vannere) was able to watch the Becket pilgrims pouring over Blackheath to Canterbury.

As to the river, it was trade with the continent rather than local fishery that concerned Greenwich seamen. Wyngaerde's drawings, made in 1558, show a waterfront with wharves, ramps and boatsheds, and a clutch of dinghies at the jetty. This was no doubt the pattern from very early times; everybody who could used the river, and the inhabitants must have been natural watermen. Doings of individual ships and their owners stud the records. In 1229 a Greenwich mariner is licensed to trade to Gascony; the Greenwich ship, *La Mighele,* master and crew officially armed, is selected to sail with four others against a Scottish rising of 1319; in June 1343 *La Cristemasse* of Greenwich, master William Meller, is among 300 ships arrested for mutiny and desertion—leaving Edward III's army unsupported in Brittany; one cause, apparently, being that they are called out too often on the king's business to be able to attend to their own. (Merchant and royal navies having largely to double for each other, the dual role was acceptable only so long as neither half of it continued past reason.) But the penalty, whatever it was, did not prevent John Meller, William's heir, possessing a house worth ten silver marks in Greenwich in 1417.

In an age when men liked to see things as simply good or

simply wicked, Humphrey Plantagenet was too complicated a character to be wholly acceptable to his contemporaries. He was that rare combination, delightful to watch if uncomfortable to be near, the intellectual mind in the man of action. A brilliant soldier, master of the art of siege, he could be brave to the point of recklessness in the field, as careless of his own safety as he was concerned for the welfare of his men. Yet sometimes he has incurred the charge of cowardice. Scholar and seeker after great thought, he could himself be childishly irrational. Chivalrous and passionate as he was, even in his own London among the ordinary citizens who adored him, there was dismay and censure over his cold treatment of his first wife. When he married her, Jacqueline of Hainault was already married uncongenially to the Duke of Brabant—a marriage which Humphrey tried for six unsuccessful years to have annulled before he accepted defeat and married his mistress, Eleanor Cobham. But the impetuosity, lusty spending of himself, much of the ambition, the confidence, some of the patriotic fervour, even a little of the gaiety, had left him by the time he came to Greenwich. The rose-pink palace by the Thames was the creation of a brilliant but slowed-up man, the achievement of his maturity.

Bella Court on its fabulous site was, and was intended to be, physically luxurious, intellectually superb. Architecturally, it does not appear to have made very much of a sensation. There were few capitals of northern Europe that Humphrey did not know, and, expert as he was in the art of knocking down great buildings, that alert mind of his must have acquired a wrinkle or two as to how to put them up. Perhaps one may regret that he had no campaigns in Italy: that, unlike a later possessor of Greenwich, he had no Inigo Jones to bring back a classic. With a sudden quiver of excitement we do find him writing to his agent in Italy, Pier Candido Decembrio, asking him to procure the definitive treatise on classical architecture by Vitruvius; but alas, the date was 1439, and the new palace at Greenwich by then not only designed but built.

The house was clothed in embroidery and jewels. But most of all it was furnished with books. These books were destined for the university at Oxford, and even now it is only professional scholars who know how much we owe to Humphrey. Fourteenth-century Oxford was not without books; the monks of Durham had set up a library on the site of Trinity College; several single works, some from Henry V, had been donated; and in 1327 Thomas Cobham, Bishop of Worcester, had bequeathed some volumes of his own to the university. But these books were few, and so rare that they had to be chained in the solar above the congregation house; only very occasionally might one of them be borrowed against pledges by the masters, and pupils were quite unable to take them away for any sort of private study. More relevant, the content of these volumes was largely a matter of chance; no benefactor had thought to comb the knowledge of Europe for its written learning.

This, Humphrey set out to do. It has not been analysed which books he wanted for his own private reading, which he selected as a basis for the instruction of the scholars at Oxford. Some of the commissions he gave in Italy for the translation into Latin of Greek classics seem designed specifically for the university library; others may have been passed on as likely to be valuable to the students only after he had enjoyed them himself. What is certain is that, even more than his munificent patronage, his grasp of what constituted essential learning was what made his gifts of books so supremely important. Definitive treatises on history, geography, philosophy, agriculture, medicine, astronomy and the arts—if they did not exist then Humphrey ordered them to be written. The whole foundation of what should be taught was laid down through his initiative.

William Caxton set up the first English printing press at Westminster in the 1470s, and the day of the hand-written book was ended. But it was during the half century or so in which

Humphrey's volumes were the chief repository of written knowledge at Oxford that the pattern of scholarship there was set;
this learning was what the masters now taught their pupils, and
these books would be among the earliest to be printed. No
scholar who went to Oxford after Humphrey's first gift could
remain uninfluenced by the magnanimity of his mind. By land
or water, most of Humphrey's books came first to Greenwich:
precious volumes bound in jewelled velvet or tooled with gold
on leather. But of course it was the contents that mattered.
He wrote to his agent, Candido, on 23 March 1439, thanking
him for five volumes of Plato's *Republic*: 'Do not think that
anything can give us more pleasure than that which relates to
learning. . . . We possess Livy and other eminent writers, and
nearly all the works of Cicero which have been hitherto found.
If you have anything of great value, we beg of you to tell us.'

It was not only the classical writers who engaged Humphrey's
attention; those three harbingers of the Renaissance, Dante,
Petrarch and Boccaccio, were well represented. Nor was all the
reading serious; his secretary, Antonio di Beccaria, who translated
Boccaccio for him as well as Athanasius, also himself wrote erotic
poetry. And the Italians were not the only ones to benefit from
his patronage; among many men of letters in England, the
poet John Lydgate received a number of commissions from
Humphrey; another English poet, George Assheby, was for a
time one of his servants.

John Capgrave, who called Humphrey 'the most lettered prince
in the world', produced his *Chronicle of England* at the duke's
behest; and the Italian scholar Titus Livius forsook his own land
to join his household; it was he to whom Humphrey entrusted
the writing of his brother's memorial, the *Vita Henrici Quinti*.
To the palace at Greenwich came not only the greatest intellects
of the day, or works representing them, but the admiration of
the world for so wide and wise an interest in scholarship.
Humphrey's present of 129 books made to Oxford in 1439 was

'a more splendid donation than any prince or king had given since the foundation of the University'. Parliament itself was urged to make him a public expression of thanks. The house by the Thames must have seemed, to Englishmen at any rate, the centre of the civilised world—more princely than any rival establishment the dull king and his ambitious wife could sponsor. Once the bitter, jealous idea had taken root that Humphrey could not be emulated, it was only a short step to suggesting that this man, already since 1435 heir to his nephew's throne, might have in his mind to usurp it.

Even now, historical documents of the time give off a vapour of the loathing many of his contemporaries, and particularly the queen, felt for Humphrey. (Was it Gibbon who said all history is hatred or flattery?) He is called greedy, grasping, debauched, cowardly and unpatriotic. His actions belie the accusations; this was the man who married his mistress as soon as his first impractical marriage had been annulled; who brought up his two illegitimate children in honour and affection; who for much of his youth lived the hard, austere life of the professional soldier; who was regarded in Europe—critical in such matters—as the bravest in the field besides being the most brilliant; who voluntarily accepted a salary cut to a token £1,000 a year during the stringent financial times of 1433; whose outbursts of political rage were directed against a supine Council activated, as he saw it, by what would nowadays be called defeatism; whose vast benefactions were inspired as much by his sense of the need of the nation as by the fashionable wish for personal fame. To quote his protégé, John Lydgate, who translated into English for him Boccaccio's *Fall of Princes*: 'Word is but wind: leave word and take the deed.' From Humphrey's deeds Oxford got the Bodleian Library; from the deeds of Margaret of Anjou, England got the Wars of the Roses.

But Margaret of Anjou got Greenwich. The annexation, long drawn out but inexorable, was not, of course, entirely her own.

As early as 1441 Humphrey's enemies, the Beauforts, had tried to damage him through his wife; and long before that date his actions had been fettered by their hatred. Eleanor Cobham was the daughter of Sir Reynold de Cobham (1381–1446), son of the 2nd Lord Cobham and Eleanor Colepeper; some mystery hangs about Sir Reynold's origins, for, in an age when honours were seized upon, he never took the title. His daughter's claims to gentility were openly said to be spurious; the writer Waurin, who being an observer of many of Humphrey's European campaigns was in some position to comment, said of her that she was 'a woman of low estate'—too low, at any rate, for a prince of the blood royal. The chronicler Edward Hall wrote: 'If he were unquieted with his other pretensed wife, truly he was ten times more vexed by occasion of this woman, so that he began his marriage with evil and ended it with worse.'

Whatever her beginnings, Eleanor was loved by her husband —his biographer, K. H. Vickers, describes her as 'the passion of his life'—and she proved an accomplished chatelaine of the house at Greenwich. Said to be of great beauty, she won the affection of the young king, her husband's ward, and received presents and honours at his hand. A note survives of the New Year gifts sent to Greenwich by Henry in 1437, when Humphrey received 'a tabulet of gold, with an image of oure Ladye hanging by three cheynes', and set with pearls, diamonds and sapphires. Eleanor's gift was 'a brouche maad in manner of a man garnished with a fayre great ball', and also adorned with pearls, diamonds and rubies. In the previous year she had been accoladed with the robes of the Order of the Garter, and invited to keep the feast of St George at Windsor.

Eleanor shared in many of Humphrey's intellectual activities; in particular, she was interested in astrology, a science which readily turned to necromancy and the study of the black arts. Or so said her accusers; for this was a chink in Humphrey's defences through which his enemies suddenly saw that they might attack. In July 1441, two priests found guilty of that abominable offence, making a waxen image of the king and watching it melt away, confessed in a blaze of publicity that they had done this thing at the instigation of the Duchess of Glouces-ter. Tried before a commission convened by the Archbishop of Canterbury (who, however, excused himself from appearing), Eleanor denied the treason while admitting an interest in the black arts.

A finding of guilt was inevitable; her penance public and humiliating. There was in it all the pleasure of pride toppled —Humphrey had been Protector of England for more than a decade; his duchess was, after all, the first lady in the land— and any action against her struck at her husband. Clad only in a shift—'Farewelle, damask and clothes of gold'—bareheaded and with 'a meek and demure countenance', carrying candle offer-ings for the altars of Christchurch at Aldgate, St Michael's, Corn-hill, and the high altar at St Paul's, Eleanor was sentenced to take three long walks through the city of London, that city whose inhabitants had so often and so loudly shouted: 'Good Duke Humphrey!' The mayor of London, sheriffs, officers of the city guilds, all good friends of Humphreys', were ordered to escort her in the penance; afterwards she was to be confined to prison for life. The young king, it was said, had pleaded against the death penalty, and it may well have been thought that lifelong im-prisonment would be the more damaging to her husband.

There is a curious objectivity in accounts of Eleanor's fall. Undoubtedly it caused a great sensation. *Lament of the Duchess of Gloucester*, by an unknown contemporary, with its haunting refrain, 'Alle women may be ware by me', remains one of the most quoted poems of the period. But although the public may have felt awe and horror at her fate, the emotions of both her judges and her husband seem curiously muted, as if—like the documents concerning Humphrey's death—some editor has been busy exorcising all passion. Humphrey has been accused of apathy in the face of his wife's disgrace; but it is hard to see what he might have done. For a time, obviously, his enemies had triumphed. The young king's affections were now completely alienated; and Gloucester must have realised that he himself might not have to wait long for an accusation of treachery.

He still attended the Council, still took part in the government of the kingdom. Nor did he hesitate to speak his patriotic mind. When the question of Henry's marriage came up, it was Gloucester who urged that the national advantage lay in a union with a daughter of John, Count of Armagnac, an old ally of the English and one who had helped to contain the ambitions of France. A different policy triumphed. An alliance friendly to the French, it was felt by the Beaufort party, might soften French enmity and bring an end to the choking continental wars. It was, of course, appeasement; but the deputation which went to René, Count of Anjou, to seek the hand of his daughter Margaret for their young king took word also that the chief opponent in England to the marriage was likely to be the king's uncle Gloucester.

Margaret of Anjou's modern biographer, Philippe Erlanger, has told how the seeds of hatred were sown in her heart before she ever landed in England. William de la Pole, Earl of Suffolk, who stood in for Henry VI at the proxy marriage in Nancy cathedral in 1445, 'did not fail, in painting a picture of the English court for Margaret, to do so in colours which matched his own political interest. Before they had reached Normandy the young queen had already conceived a filial respect for Cardinal Beaufort of Winchester, and a strong aversion to Gloucester and his friends.'

With the queen behind them, it took less than two years for the Beaufort faction to encompass Humphrey's fall. By the end of 1446 all was ready; on 14 December writs were issued for a Parliament to meet on the next 10th of February—'the which parlement,' says an anonymous chronicle of the time, 'was made only for to slay the noble duke of Gloucestre.' It was felt necessary to summon the members to a place away from London, for there Humphrey was too well loved for harm to be done to him; and eventually Suffolk's own stronghold of Bury St Edmunds was chosen. Fearing great opposition, the conspirators assembled a force of about fifty thousand troops and deployed them round the town.

But Humphrey set out from Greenwich with a retinue of no more than eighty, 'like an innocent lamb', as one writer put it. Conscious of no treachery in himself, and hoping only to use the occasion to plead for his wife's pardon and release, he came unsuspecting to Bury. The story—how he proceeded through the ill-omened alley called Dead Lane to his lodgings; how, after a message from the king that he was not to present himself at the court 'because of the cold', he ate his dinner alone and was then arrested; how the next morning he was found in his prison cell paralysed and near death—is well known.

Humphrey, Duke of Gloucester, died at about three o'clock on the afternoon of Tuesday, 23 February 1447. On Wednesday, 24 February, Parliament had placed before it Margaret's plans to take over the bulk of Humphrey's manors; one week later, on 3 March, a bill was passed depriving his widow of any rights in his estate. Even before his last breath had been drawn, the scramble for his brilliant heritage had begun; by the fatal Tuesday itself, a grant of some of his revenues had already been made to Henry VI's foundation of King's College, Cambridge. And well before Easter Queen Margaret of Anjou was in possession at Greenwich.

CHAPTER 6

Plesaunce and the Roses

Margaret of Anjou's establishment of herself in Duke Humphrey's palace at Greenwich was childish—but then she was a child. This greedy, jealous girl was no more than fifteen when she married Henry VI, seventeen by the time she obtained Greenwich. Her first action was to change the name : 'Plesaunce,' say the 1447 accounts, 'the Queen's park, late Bellacourte'. Next, she ordered new glass for the windows, glass 'fluoshyd', in the old phrase, 'cum margaritis'—those daisies which had been everywhere at the Nancy wedding, strewn underfoot, incorporated in the metal pattern on the shields of the soldiers, embroidered on the hangings of balconies, on banners, sewn with silver and gold thread all over the white satin wedding dress of the fifteen-year-old bride. Strange that this queen, so bitter, so masculine, should be so closely associated with daisies and roses.

There is no doubt that Margaret loved Greenwich. Over a period of five years her embellishments to the palace were extensive and continuous. The accounts of Robert Ketewell, 'Clerk of the Quenyswerkys of the maner of Plesaunce'—a local man who was to spend his life in the service of Plesaunce and to be buried by the side of his wife Agnes in the churchyard of St Alfege—list a vast proliferation of new courts and pavilions, stretches of pavement, wainscotting, bay windows—the last multitudinously glazed with the queen's emblem. We know that the house was of pink brick and ivory-white stone; those people who were engaged in the archaeological digs of 1970 and 1971 were struck most, I think, by the beauty of positive colour—this palace of pink and white, roses and daisies, on its golden gravel strand, the crystal river flowing by, past a park of apple–green grass and bottle-green trees, under a wide blue and white sky.

One of Margaret's prime preoccupations was the enrichment of her own apartments. Ketewell's accounts note that her chamber was to be paved with Flanders tiles, that a great new door was to be fixed to it, and a tresans, or dais, was to be built at the higher end; the door was ornamented with two hundred tin nails (called in the accounts 'dicehednayles'), and its tin double hinges weighed $75\frac{1}{2}$lb. For 5s a vessel called a bathing vat was supplied, 'in which the Queen—', and a state bed, costing 8s 6d, was delivered from London. Of particular interest to ourselves was the pair of beds ordered from Richard Henham, the Greenwich carpenter; they cost 4s each and were fixed by him 'in the lodging within the little garden for the King's brothers'. These two boys were Edmund and Jasper, sons of the marriage between the king's widowed mother and her Welsh squire, Owen Tudor.

We do not know how the news of Humphrey's murder—for such it was widely accepted to be—first came to Greenwich. There must have been a panic-stricken messenger riding through the dark, bringing tidings not only of the death of the lord of the manor, but of the arrest of some forty-two of his followers. Five of these, including his illegitimate son, Arthur, were actually hanged, their bodies already marked for the quartering—but cut down alive in a dramatic last-minute reprieve arranged, as some said, in a bid for their own popularity by the murderers.

Among those implicated in Humphrey's death, three men were held to be primarily responsible. They were William de la Pole, Earl of Suffolk, Adam Moleyns, priest, and Sir James Fiennes. In a sequence of events that helps to illuminate the 500-year-old reputation for love of justice enjoyed by Englishmen, all these three were eventually brought to judgement—not by the judicial processes of the law but by the people. It took three

years: years during which the mounting disasters in France, the
oppressions at home, the manifest improprieties of Margaret and
her ministers, all fulfilled too exactly the abuses against which
Humphrey had warned so passionately, to allow his memory to
rest. Suddenly, in 1450, the anger exploded. Adam Moleyns,
who had been prosecuting counsel at the trial of Eleanor Gloucester and was now become Bishop of Chichester and Lord Privy
Seal, went to Portsmouth on 9 January and was killed by the
sailors there. In April, William de la Pole, now Duke of Suffolk,
was impeached by Parliament and, for his own safety, banished
by Henry VI. The ship taking him to France was intercepted on
1 May by the *Nicholas of the Tower*. Suffolk was ordered to
come aboard, tried by a court set up by the officers and crew,
found guilty of, among other things, causing the death of Duke
Humphrey, and beheaded, his body being later cast up on the
beach at Dover. There remained Sir James Fiennes, now Lord
Saye and Sele—that man who had been given the old West
Greenwich title on the very day of Humphrey's death, along
with his offices of Constable of Dover and Warden of the Cinque
Ports.

Unlike Wat Tyler, who had led his workmates pouring over
Blackheath into London some seventy years earlier in a protest
against brutal taxes, Jack Cade and his followers were not concerned with money. Theirs was a mission of justice, in which the
punishment of murderers and the removal of wicked men
wrongly in control of the kingdom was at least as important an
aim as any complaint about unjust taxation. Shakespeare's in-
dictment of these 'rebellious hinds, the filth and scum of Kent,
mark'd for the gallows' could scarcely have been wider of the
target.

The lists of those who assembled with Jack Cade on Blackheath on 1 June 1450 make fascinating local reading. The one
knight, Sir John Cheyne, of Eastchurch, Sheppey, had ridden
with Humphrey, Duke of Gloucester, to the fatal Parliament at

Bury, and had been among those arrested there. Robert Poy-
nings, referred to in the records as Cade's 'carver and sewer', was
a descendant of the Rokesleys. Of the eighteen esquires, Thomas
Ballard was a Greenwich landowner and neighbour of Humphrey; his family had held the manor of Combe since Gregory
Ballard, butler to Richard II, had been granted it in 1396.
Gregory, attended by three local bowmen, had set out with
Humphrey for Agincourt, but had lost his life at the siege of
Harfleur. The several Culpepers were kinsmen of Eleanor Cobham. William Haute, a Greenwich tenant of the abbot of Ghent,
had for wife Jane Widville of Lee.

Of the seventy-four gentlemen in the Cade lists, Thomas
Hethe of Woolwich was a substantial local resident who must
have been known to Humphrey; and the same might be said of
William Northampton, Woolwich lawyer. John Stone was of
Deptford, a tenant of the old Says. The Chesemans, several of
whom appear in the lists, were an old and important family of
the manor of Greenwich, holding several tenancies from Ghent;
they had control of many of the woods in this thickly wooded
area, and had also from time to time collected rents for the
abbot. Almost certainly they had served Duke Humphrey.

A man known to have worked at the palace was Richard
Henham, the Greenwich carpenter who had made the beds for
the Tudor princes. His wife, Margery, figures with him in the
lists, and there were other Greenwich wives implicated with
their husbands, women like Margery Gate, wife of the butcher,
John Gate; Petronilla Fox, wife of Richard Fox, described as a
labourer, who had helped to lay some of the Plesaunce paving;
Margaret, wife of the couper, John Berde; Petronilla Nele, wife
of Simon Nele, the poulter; Margery, wife of Nicholas Astyng,
tailor; Alicia Denys, wife of the baker, Radus Denys. Possibly
these women were helping their husbands to feed and shelter the
rebels during their encampment on Blackheath. Other local
people concerned were the yeomen, John Cokke—the Cokkes, or

Cokes, owned land near Billingsgate dock—John Crabbe and
Radus Yonge, of Plumstead; Robert Ricard, mariner, of the
same place; Bernard Cabell, Constable of the Hundred of Rokes-
ley and father-in-law of Robert Cheseman; William Ederiche
and his wife Alicia, who had sold a substantial property in East
Greenwich to the Chesemans and Henry Newark in 1434; Henry
Newark himself, and his wife Margaretta; Edmund Ryculf of
Lee, Constable of the Hundred of Blackheath.

It is also worth noting the character of those involved in the
assassinations which ushered in the Cade rebellion. The Portsmouth seamen who murdered Adam Moleyns had served under
Humphrey, ferrying him to several of his campaigns. The sailors
who manned the *Nicholas of the Tower* must have known him;
they were almost certainly recruited from this stretch of the
Thames. This was one of the ships that had conveyed Henry V's
army to France in 1415—William Robinson, its master, was a
member of a local family which was to have a very long and
proud association with Greenwich and the navy. A comparison
of the list of John Cade's followers with that of Humphrey's
retinue in the French wars shows that a substantial number of
these men, or their fathers, fought with him at Agincourt; and
more of them, or their sons, were to support his protégé, the
Duke of York, against Henry VI and Margaret of Anjou in the
Wars of the Roses.

Perhaps it was this feeling, that Humphrey's manor was at the
heart of the rebellion, that made Henry and Margaret indulge in
a vindictive humiliation of the people of Greenwich. The climax
of Cade's march on London had been the execution of Lord Saye
and Sele, the third of Humphrey's murderers. After this act, as
many would see it, of judicial retribution, the rebels expressed
themselves willing to accept a pardon and return home. This
pardon was duly negotiated with them at Southwark on 7 July
1450, by the crown's representatives, Henry himself being careful to keep away. It was not quite the end. There was to be the

miserable pursuit and death of Cade himself, followed by a frenzied posthumous beheading and the dispatch of one of his quarters to Blackheath. And during the next six months a trickle of executions of citizens at Canterbury and Rochester was designed to mark the length of the king's arm.

On 23 February 1451 took place what the royal occupants of Plesaunce must have hoped would be the final act in the affair, when, as Stow put it, 'Henry at Blackheath made the men of Kent resident in that neighbourhood do humble penance for their bold daring of the previous summer. Naked, save for their shirts, they met the King and asked pardon on their knees.' There was more than an echo of the humiliation of Eleanor Cobham about it all.

Of course it was not the end but a beginning. Richard, Duke of York, had been Humphrey's ward and was to become his avenger. (One of his first actions as Protector was to petition Parliament to clear Gloucester's name of the charge of treachery which had lain on it since the infamous arrest at Bury in 1447.) It is no surprise to find that the first attempt by the Yorkists to rally opposition against Henry VI and his hated queen was made at Blackheath. Here, in February 1452, within a spear's throw of Humphrey's palace, assembled a small but enthusiastic force prepared to face the king in what was virtually the first confrontation between Red Rose and White. It did not come to blows; Henry was malleable, and the two sides backed away. The tents were taken down, the armour unbuckled; butcher and baker, cooper, poulter, yeoman, gentleman and knight retired temporarily to their homes.

This is not the place to set down a chronicle of the Wars of the Roses. As the rival fortunes ebb and flow, Greenwich may be seen as a prize in the game rather than a place of combat. Here in 1455, after an agonised Lancastrian period of some eighteen months during which Henry VI had been in a state of total withdrawal from the world, at a meeting on 7 March, held 'in a

certain chapel over the gate at Greenwich', Margaret of Anjou
announced to a startled Council that the Protectorate headed by
the Duke of York was over, and that the king was once again in
command of his own realm. Here, two months later, she sat with
her little son Edward, born on 13 October 1453, waiting for news
of the campaign that was to culminate in the battle of St Albans.
As things went worse and worse for the Lancastrians, Greenwich, with its overstated daisies, its nostalgic memories of Good
Duke Humphrey, became too unreliable a shelter, and Margaret
and her son sought a surer sanctuary in Lancastrian country in the
north. Later still, a triumphant Edward of York, crowned Edward
IV, made an entry into Plesaunce that must have been as joyful
an occasion for the town as it was for himself. That was in
October 1461; he came, says Sir James Ramsay in his *Lancaster
and York*, after the coronation and the provincial progress, because here he was able to indulge his love of the chase. But he
must, surely, have come as well to enjoy the fervour of these, his
most ardent supporters. Among his guests for the hunting was
an emissary from the court of Francesco Sforza, Duke of Milan,
whose predecessor, Duke Philippo Mario Visconti, had been
among Humphrey's most eminent Italian correspondents. It must
have seemed to many a local man that the avowed aim of the
Yorkists—restoration of the days of Good Duke Humphrey—
was about to be achieved.

A terrible disillusion was in store. On 1 May 1464 the king
made a secret marriage. The bride was a local beauty, Elizabeth
Widville, daughter of Sir Richard Widville of the manor of Lee.
Through her mother she had other local connections; Jacquetta
of Luxembourg was a daughter of the Count of St Pol, that
comté of French Flanders which had provided lords of the manor
of Combe for most of the thirteenth century. Jacquetta, herself a
great beauty, had after the death of her first husband—Humphrey's brother John, Duke of Bedford—consoled her widowhood by marrying a man '*renommé d'estre le plus beau Chevalier*

que l'en sceust nulle part', in the words of the French commentator, Monstrelet. It was not surprising that their daughter should have inherited looks to melt the heart of a king.

The Widville family had been originally of Grafton, Northamptonshire. Richard Widville senior entered the service of Henry IV very young, perhaps as a boy companion to the heir to the throne. William Paston quotes the Earl of Warwick as saying that he was brought up with Henry V and he has been described as his squire of the body. Later he joined the retinue of the king's brother, Thomas, Duke of Clarence, and later still served with the Duke of Bedford in France. He was present at meetings of the Council and must have heard Humphrey of Gloucester's passionate arguments for firmness in the French dealings. His daughter Jane married that William Haute who had fought with Humphrey at Agincourt and was to stand with Jack Cade on Blackheath.

Richard Widville, his son, became the husband of the widowed Duchess of Bedford in 1436; in the same year he was in the service of the Earl of Suffolk and went with him to France. Again in attendance on Suffolk, Richard Widville the younger was present at the proxy marriage with Margaret of Anjou at Nancy in 1444, and was one of those who escorted the French bride to England. His wife's sister Isabel had married Charles, Count of Maine—Margaret of Anjou's uncle; and Widville must have been among those whose advice, so angering the patriots, had led to the cession of Maine and Anjou to France in 1446. This man could never have seemed anything but a traitor to Duke Humphrey. Worse locally, he was one of the most vigorous prosecutors of Jack Cade and the Kent rebels.

Walter of Douai's Domesday manor of Lee had become subdivided and confused after its return to Ghent in 1222, less effective than it should have been as a reinforcement of the defences of the Thames. Its acquisition by the Duke of Bedford in 1425, acting in some sort of conjunction with the Widvilles, was perhaps part of the military precaution which was prompting the crown to strengthen its overall holding in Greenwich after the final dispossesion of Ghent. By marriage with Bedford's widow, young Richard Widville gained a double title to the manor of Lee, and in 1438 he and his bride took possession from that old courtier and one-time guardian of the Fair Maid of Kent, Sir Richard Sturry. It was possibly here that their eldest child, Elizabeth, was born.

Less than a year after his marriage to Elizabeth Widville, Edward IV granted her 'the lordship and manor of Plesaunce, otherwise called of Grenewiche, with the Tower of Grenewiche and the parks there, to be held by the Queen for her life, as amply as by Humph. late Duke of Gloucester'. Perhaps it was meant as a conciliatory gesture to the local people; if so, it was a tactless, damaging one. Elizabeth was no stranger to the palace; apart from having been brought up in the neighbourhood she had been in the service of Queen Margaret of Anjou, high in her affection, a lady of the bedchamber. The looks which had ensnared their young king (by magic, it was said, engendered by the foreign woman, her mother) were less likely here than anywhere in England to sue for forgiveness. Seeing that pretty Lancastrian face in Humphrey's corridors, Greenwich people must have felt bitterly betrayed.

The Wars of the Roses were not, of course, ended; the king's marriage helped to prolong them. Observed from our distance, Elizabeth Widville seems to have shown an altogether incomprehensible insensitivity to the damage she caused to the York image. Her advocacy of honours for her family went far beyond reasonableness; the diligence with which she diverted York patronage to people who had all too recently been the king's enemies, in this place above all was not likely to be endurable. A climax came in 1466, when on 1 October Greenwich witnessed a wedding arranged by the queen between Thomas Grey, her son by her first husband, the ardent Lancastrian Lord Ferrers of Groby, and Anne, daughter and heiress of the Duke of Exeter. But Anne was already betrothed to the nephew of Richard Neville, Earl of Warwick—Warwick the Kingmaker, to whom the House of York owed all they had, not excluding the English crown. Obsessed with maternal ambition, Elizabeth had actually paid the Duchess of Exeter four thousand marks to break the pre-contract with Warwick's nephew. It was the first real intimation—not only for Warwick but for those countless men who had ventured everything they had for the White Rose—that the goal was not reached: that a greedy, jealous woman could still annihilate Duke Humphrey's justice.

Less than other people can princes afford ingratitude. There came a day when Warwick could no longer stomach the distorted scale of values that placed any Lancastrian Widville above every loyal follower of York. Margaret of Anjou was contacted in her lonely castle of Koeur, near Verdun; armies were raised. And the civil war was on again.

It could not last; in spite of some initial Lancastrian successes it was the York rose that flourished. After capture, escape and flight to Burgundy, Edward was able to return with an army strong enough to beat Warwick at the Battle of Barnet, and to leave the Kingmaker dead on the field. Three weeks later, the Battle of Tewkesbury killed Margaret's son, Edward, Prince of Wales. Henry VI, quiet cause of all the trouble, was quietly murdered in the Tower. And at last, for Edward IV at any rate, there was no one left to fight.

Elizabeth's fortitude in the face of great tribulation had not gone unnoticed. Fair-minded Englishmen finally conceded that her bearing, the courage with which she had awaited the birth of the heir to the throne (Edward V, born in sanctuary at Westminster, his father defeated and in exile, his mother all but destitute), the steady protection she had afforded throughout the wars to the king's children, the unflinching loyalty she had shown him and his cause, made her a fit consort for him. In the very last, most critical days of the war, when, as Waurin wrote, 'the Qwene, my lord Prince and my ladies her doghtars . . . was likely to stand in the grettest ioperdy that evar they stode', her bravery in the Tower of London, from which she must have been able to see the enemy's advance, the burning of London Bridge, the inexorable approach—only halted by the equally calm courage of her brother, Anthony Widville, Lord Rivers, who sallied forth from a postern gate and repulsed the soldiers of Fauconberg—all this touched the hearts of the people of England, and on 13 October 1472 she was publicly praised for her constancy by the Speaker of the House of Commons, William Alynton.

> O quene Elizabeth, o Blessed creature,
> O glorious God, what payne had she—

as a political poem of the time, 'Recovery of the Throne by Edward IV', put it.

On this same day Louis de Gruthuyse, Seigneur of Bruges, Prince of Steenhuyse, the Burgundian Governor of Holland and a good friend of Edward's, who had been of material help in his efforts to regain his throne, was rewarded by the earldom of Winchester. Gruthuyse had been invited to England to receive the king's honour, and to meet a grateful queen; and a series of magnificent entertainments was arranged at Windsor and Westminster, after which he was brought to the queen's manor of Greenwich. An anonymous account by an Englishman in his train sets the scene: 'Then, about nine of the clock, the King and Queen, with her ladies and gentlewomen, brought the said Lord Grauthuse to three chambers of Plesaunce, all hanged with white silk and linen cloth, and all the floors covered with carpets. There was ordained a bed for him, selve [alone], of as good down as could be gotten, the sheets of Rennes, also fine fustians; the counterpane cloth of gold, furred with ermine, the tester and celer also shining cloth of gold, the curtains of white sarcenet; as for his head suit and pillows they were of the Queen's own ordonnance.' In the second chamber there was another state bed, 'the which was all white. Also in the same chamber was made a couch with feather beds, hanged with a tent knit like a net, and there was a cupboard.' Two baths stood in the third chamber, covered with tents of white cloth. When Gruthuyse and his lord chamberlain 'had been in their baths as long as was their pleasure, they had green ginger, divers syrups, comfits and ipocras, and then they went to bed. And on the morn, he took his leave of the King and Queen, and turned to Westminster again.'

In 1483, Elizabeth Widville's tenure of the manor of Greenwich came to a sudden and calamitous end. On 23 April of that year, at the age of forty, Edward IV died—and the world of the Widvilles died with him. Anthony Widville, Lord Rivers, the queen's brother, and Richard Haute, her cousin, had been put in charge of the establishment of the young Prince of Wales at Ludlow; and as soon as the news reached there of his father's death, Widville and Haute took steps to bring the little king to London. On 29 April they reached Stony Stratford where they met Richard, Duke of Gloucester. Widville, Haute and the queen's second son, Sir Richard Grey, who was with them, were seized and taken to Pontefract, where they were executed. The little king was hurried to London, to the Tower, from which he was never to emerge.

There follow the turbulent two years of Richard III's reign, during which another Cade-like rebellion bursts out, with many of the same families taking part. Could inspiration be said any longer to lie in the rule of Good Duke Humphrey? It was almost forty years since Gloucester's murder, and two dynasties had come and gone. It is a measure of the strength of feeling of Kent men—the obstinacy if you like—that yet again they were willing to risk everything they had in the name of justice.

At the head of the rising of 1483 was Henry Stafford, Duke of Buckingham, who, it has been said, raised the standard of revolt as soon as he learned of the murder of the two young princes in the Tower. The boys were his nephews, since he was married to Katherine Widville, sister of the queen. Two of her brothers, Richard and Edward Widville, both followed Buckingham on his errand of revenge. Richard Widville their father had been that character most detestable to the British, a turncoat. But his sons had embraced wholeheartedly the Yorkist cause. Anthony Widville, Lord Rivers, the eldest, had been a brave and loyal subject to his brother-in-law, eventually giving his life for the White Rose. (He was a cultivated man; we may note that he aspired to succour learning on the Gloucester scale—in one sense more successfully, since he was the patron of Caxton.)

Hautes rose; the Haute contingent was led by Sir William Haute, brother of the executed Richard. With him were his son, also Richard, and Sir John Fogg, a Kent man who had married one of the Haute daughters. Sir John Cheyne was there, son of Duke Humphrey's squire. Anthony Kene, of Well Hall, Eltham, was the eldest son of William Kene, sheriff of Kent; Sir Thomas Lewknor, a kinsman of the Colepepers (who were also there), held lands in Eltham; William Strode came of a family owning houses in Mottingham and Woolwich; John Hoo, described as a yeoman, seems to have been the son of the rector of St Margaret's, Lee; his friend Richard Potter was probably the son of the vicar of Deptford, who bore the same name. There must have been many other local men in the rising, whose names have not come down to us, tenants of the Widvilles at Lee, sons of families who had served Humphrey at Bella Court, Greenwich citizens who could not stomach the non-righting of wrongs.

This time the rebels did not assemble on Blackheath. The Widville country house was at The Mote, Maidstone; that of the Hautes was another famous Mote, the one at Ightham. To these two estates secretly went the men of Kent, determined once again to punish murderers in high places. 18 October was the day appointed for the rising, and it was planned to break out simultaneously all over southern Britain. Early on that day the

Duke of Buckingham raised his standard at Brecknock, in Wales; the queen's eldest son, the Marquis of Dorset, was to rouse the men of Exeter; Lionel Widville, another brother of the queen, and bishop of Salisbury, was to raise a force there; Hautes, Widvilles and their Kent followers were to rally at Maidstone.

The rebellion was defeated before it had begun— and not by Richard III. A cruel act of weather—a terrible rainstorm—blew up. Torrential downpours flooded the Severn and barred Buckingham's progress out of Wales. Dorset was unable to move from Exeter. Henry, Earl of Richmond, who was to have reinforced the army assembling on the south coast with his own substantial following from Brittany, had his fleet so dispersed by gales at sea that several transports including his own only narrowly avoided shipwreck and had to run to Normandy for shelter. Buckingham was captured and beheaded. Most of the other leaders fled and were able to join Henry in Brittany. Here, on Christmas Day 1483, in return for a solemn oath made in Rennes cathedral whereby Henry Tudor vowed to marry Edward IV's eldest daughter, Elizabeth of York, now heiress to the English throne, the rebels promised him their fullest support. By 1 August 1485 they were ready again; before the end of that month the battle of Bosworth Field had clinched the matter.

It is not possible here to go into the argument raised by some twentieth-century historians against the probability that Richard III murdered his nephews. All one can say is that without doubt his contemporaries at Greenwich, the ordinary men and women of the Hundred of Blackheath, thought he did. They thought this without any prompting from the Tudors. They rose almost instinctively, as soon as the rumours of the princes' murder became current. They were of the same stock who had fought with Humphrey at Agincourt, had marched with Jack Cade to avenge his murder, had pursued that aim by supporting the House of York. To these local men, the vow at Rennes must have seemed as much an acclamation as an expurgation of all they had endured since 1447.

The marriage between Elizabeth, heiress of York, and Henry Tudor took place in 1486. A small, subtle poem was written soon afterwards by an unknown poet in celebration; although we have no proof, there is an overwhelming sense that the setting is the queen's garden at Greenwich. It is disguised as a song, but other meanings than the simple refrain keep breaking through: the fleur-de-lys she did regret—the lost conquests of France; gent—pretty; the gillyflower—July flower, last rose of summer, termagent, a Jezebel, a wanton woman in the last stage of her good looks. Henry Lyte, the seventeenth-century botanist, spelt it gillofer, and wrote: 'We do call this flower French Marygold.' And behind all the feigned simplicity, the exhausted, exultant refrain:

> In a glorious garden green
> Saw I sitting a comely queen
> Among the flowers that fresh been.
> She gathered a flower and set between.
> The lily-white rose me thought I saw,
> The lily-white rose me thought I saw—
> And ever she sang:

> This day, day dawns,
> This gentle day, day dawns,
> This gentle day dawns,
> And I must home gone.
> This gentle day dawns,
> This day, day dawns,
> This gentle day dawns
> And we must home gone.

> In that garden be flowers of hue,
> The gillyflower gent that she well knew;

The fleur-de-lys she did enrue,
And said: 'The white rose is most true
This garden to rule by righteous law.'
The lily-white rose me thought I saw,
And ever she sang:

This day, day dawns . . .
And we must home gone.

ELIZABETHA · VXOR
HENRICI · VII ·

Elizabeth of York. She holds a white rose

CHAPTER 7

The Rise of Placentia

We now know that Henry VII razed Humphrey's palace of Bella Court—and who can wonder? The archaeological dig of 1971 showed that nothing was allowed to remain above ground, and the only use any of the structure could be put to was as bearers for the Tudor walls. Yet, among the debris the diggers of 1971 found plaster daisies, miraculously clean and perfect; and a piece of cloth of gold with a hand-rolled hem.

By destroying Humphrey's Bella Court, Henry VII inevitably invested it with legend. Because the boundaries of the park remain unchanged we know the grandeur of its setting; but no drawing of it has survived, and its appearance can only be guessed at. No such mystery attaches to Henry's own palace. The Tudor buildings are well documented by both drawings and building accounts. The main part of the fabric, red brick with white stone dressings in the manner of Hampton Court, was almost as big as that palace and, like it, formed of many different apartments laid out round three large and numberless little courts. The state and royal rooms stretched along the river front to the chapel at the eastern end. This and the great hall lie under the Queen Anne block of the present Wren palace, and how much was newly put up by Henry and how much allowed to remain from the site's earlier history cannot at present be discovered. Outside the many doors there were a great garden and a little garden, orchard, lawns, terraces; cobbled, brick-floored or stone-paved courts—one of which was a tennis court. There was a new name, Placentia.

It is not surprising that the Greenwich of the Tudors was such a roystering place; relief at the end of the fighting must have trembled on the point of lightheadedness. The war won, the palace by the river became the setting for seemingly endless parades, or parodies, of valour and nobility. The pegs on which the chivalric dream was hung were jousting, feasting, maying, dancing, singing—no doubt wenching and whoring—as if an excess of jollity now could wipe out all the harrowing years of the Wars of the Roses. There was religion in it, too; the great religious junketings, Christmas, Easter and Whitsun, once invariably passed at Westminster or Eltham, came now more and more to be celebrated here.

Yet, it was not quite over; a few places remained where the urge to rebellion was less exhausted than it was in Kent. One of these was Cornwall; and in 1497 a great press of Cornishmen had to be met and crushed by Henry VII on Blackheath. Men building the queen's barn at Greenwich left their work and ran up the hill to have a look—the first time for more than fifty years that they would have chosen to be spectators rather than participants in a scrap.

The gentlemen of Kent were there in strength, of course, supporting the king they had helped to his throne. Of the fourteen men made knights banneret on that day, 17 June, on the battlefield of Blackheath, more than half owned property in the Hundred. The slaughter of the rebels was great; at the end of the fight the bodies were all gathered together and buried under mounds, the chief of which seems to have been that later called Whitfield's Mount and used for the practice firing of mortars. People forget what they do not wish to remember; but it seems extraordinary that this mass grave should be so quickly and so completely disregarded.

The leader of the Cornishmen was James Tuchet, Lord Audley, and he paid for the failure of his rebellion with his head. Through him there was a link with the old days more poignant than perhaps his executioners appreciated. For this misguided young man, through the marriage of his father's sister Margaret with the Yorkist Sir Richard Grey, son of Humphrey's poor, illegitimate little daughter, Antigone, was a great-grand-nephew of the Duke of Gloucester himself.

The Audleys came back into favour in the next generation and built a house at the bottom of Crooms Hill, across the mouth of what is now Burney Street. They were not the only ones to choose this place as a residence. Now that the dynastic struggles were over and the Tudors had fixed Greenwich as a favourite palace, ambitious men throughout the land were busy seeking niches here for themselves. The royal complex would house some of them, in large or small suites of apartments round the southern and eastern courts. But others would see the advantage in providing homes of their own. One site for expansion was downstream of the palace along the river bank, and here now rose mansions occupied by the king's chamberlain, Charles, Earl of Worcester, and Sir William Compton, courtier and friend to Henry VIII. Farther east there was the house of John Gunthorpe, chaplain to Elizabeth Widville and her daughter, whose deanery at Wells, Somerset, is still one of the architectural delights of that city.

West of Placentia were other mansions; one, with eight acres of grounds, was Copped Hall, a substantial place now under the west wing of the National Maritime Museum. It stood on the north side of Heath Gate Street, which was the road to Woolwich later to achieve notoriety by running so oddly through the Queen's House; and it had not only gardens and an orchard but a vineyard. Rented in the time of James I by the Cromptons, it was almost certainly the scene of the disastrous clandestine marriage of Lady Arabella Stuart; but in the early sixteenth century it belonged to the Ropers. John Roper had married Margery, half-sister of the brothers Kene—both Buckingham rebels—and their son, William Roper, was to marry Margaret, daughter of Sir Thomas More.

But the grandest house in Greenwich after the king's was the great Swanne House, built on the site of the present market. The swan was the badge of the Bohuns; Humphrey, Duke of Gloucester, whose mother was the Bohun co-heiress, had been known as the Swan or, more affectionately locally, as 'our great gander'. Swanne House belonged to the Courtenays, and their Bohun connection is traceable to the marriage in 1325 between Hugh Courtenay (1303–77), 10th Earl of Devon, and Margaret, daughter of Humphrey de Bohun, Earl of Hereford, and granddaughter of Edward I. It would be of great interest to Greenwich historians if proof could be found that the Swanne House was built in Edward I's reign, since that was the period when the royal residential connection with Greenwich became firmly established via the Rokesleys.

The Courtenay family were loyal servants of the crown through many generations; Hugh Courtenay, 11th Earl, was one of the founders of the Order of the Garter. They became staunch Lancastrians, and Thomas, 13th Earl, played a prominent part in suppressing the Cade rebellion. Perhaps its local implications touched his conscience, since afterwards he made attempts to mediate between Henry VI and the Duke of York, and died on such a mission in 1457. His son had no such inhibitions, fought on the Lancastrian side at the battle of Towton in 1459, was captured and beheaded. The heir, his youngest son John, was to be killed at the last battle of the Wars of the Roses, that of Tewkesbury, again fighting on the Lancastrian side.

The next heir was Edward Courtenay, son of a cadet branch of the family from Devon. Banished by Richard III, he had joined Henry, Earl of Richmond, in the fateful August of 1485, and had been present with him at the battle of Bosworth Field, where his valour brought restoration of the family honours. His heir, William, then a boy of twelve, was created a Knight of the Bath at the coronation of Henry's queen, Elizabeth of York, and was taken into her retinue. He fell in love with her younger sister, Katherine, and in 1495 he married her. This was an indiscretion —Katherine was being saved for a diplomatic marriage with a prince of Scotland—and his new brother-in-law, the king, had him attainted. Not until the accession of Henry VIII did he recover the favour of the Tudors, and then only partially. Although he carried the Third Sword of State at Henry VIII's coronation, only in 1511 was he made Earl of Devon. That was on 10 May; on 11 June he died of pleurisy at his house in Greenwich.

The history of the Swanne House, with its ninety-acre estate, is a saga in itself and a history of Greenwich in little. The only surviving son and heir, Henry Courtenay, Earl of Devon, revelling in the family's return to favour, was made a Knight of the Garter on 21 June 1521, High Steward of the Duchy of Cornwall, Constable of Windsor Castle, and attended his sovereign to the Field of Cloth of Gold. He was on the commission that deposed Catherine of Aragon, and helped to officiate at the trial of Anne Boleyn. Having assisted a handful of unlucky courtiers to the block, he suffered a change of mind; a lukewarm drift into rebellion resulted in his own arrest and execution on Tower Hill in 1538. Although he left heirs (the *Complete Peerage* gives a long list of them) the earldom of Devon went into dormancy with the death by poison in Italy of his son. The Swanne House, its days of glory over, passed to a succession of Greenwich speculators, becoming less and less impressive with each transfer.

One of the first to take it was Edmund Chapman, chief joiner to Elizabeth I; his interest was in the fabulous interiors. The plaster ceilings, the rich woodwork and glass were mentioned separately when he came to sell the house, and perhaps were removed. After Chapman's transfer to the Grange, in Crooms Hill, the property was in the hands of William Smith, James I's hereditary Sergeant-at-Arms, who had it divided into four tenements. By 1669 these were cut up into ten. And the last stage of the Swanne House was as a brewery, before, in 1824, it was sold to Greenwich Hospital for demolition.

But this is to race ahead; Tudor Greenwich had nothing of decline about it. Here, if not quite in Humphrey of Gloucester's pattern, in terms of richness and diplomatic grandeur was the centre of the world. Accounts of Tudor living start soberly enough, with lists of alms paid to local people who aided the king's Observances: 20s apiece to Drs Collet and Rawlens for preaching before Henry VII; alms of 6s 4d offered at Whitsun —'the usual amount' say the editors of Hasted. 'To John Rede's mariners who rode up and down singing afore the king's manor of Grenewyche, for their reward, 20s.' 'To my lord of Buckingham's players that played in the hall at Grenewich, in reward, 6s 8d.' For a man who brought a hart from Ashdown Forest there was the same amount.

It was the accession of Henry VIII, in 1509, that touched the philosopher's stone. Now the household books start to drip with a golden expenditure of fantasy and pageant. By 1511 the Christmas feast was made open to 'all respectable comers', according to the chronicler Holinshed, and the king with eleven others disguised themselves and put on an entertainment 'after the maner of Italie called a maske, a thing not seen before'. Within a year of his coronation had started the great jousts that were to be such an accompaniment to the reign. At Greenwich in the summer of 1510 the young king, still barely nineteen, issued challenges to all comers to fighting at barriers, casting the eight-foot spear, fighting with two-handed swords and with battle-axes. 'By his great strength,' commented Hall, 'the king won most praise.'

In 1512 a more elegant event took place, a three-day joust in the tilt-yard. The king broke most staves and carried off the first prize; the second, third and fourth prizes were won by the Earl of Essex, Henry Courtenay of the Swanne House, and Elizabeth Widville's grandson the Marquis of Dorset, of the manor of Lee.

In 1515, on 3 February, the king and the Marquis of Dorset 'answered all comers at joust'; Henry broke twenty-three spears and 'was highly to be praised'.

The year 1515 saw some merry-making of an intense kind at the public celebrations of the marriage of the king's sister Mary to Charles Brandon. This, on her side at least, was a love match; Mary had been the victim of a diplomatic union with the 'worn-out and decrepit' King Louis of France—her price, it was said, being marriage at his death to a lover of her own choice. At eighteen the young widow was one of the most attractive women in Europe. 'She is very beautiful,' commented an Italian diplomat at the court, 'and is without match in England. She is tall, fair, of a light complexion with a colour; gracious and graceful, a nymph from heaven.' The ambassador to the Holy Roman Empire thought 'her deportment exquisite, both in conversation and in dancing'. The only criticism found by A. F. Pollard, Henry VIII's biographer, was an Italian one that her eyes and eyebrows were too light.

This lovely young creature, '*la reine blanche*', as the French called her, chose for her second husband Charles Brandon, son of the squire Sir William Brandon, a prominent Buckingham rebel who had escaped to join Henry VII in France and had been struck down while holding his standard at the battle of Bosworth Field. His young son, Charles, had been brought up at the Tudor court, and honours, including the dukedom of Suffolk, heaped upon him for his father's sake. He had been sent to fetch the widowed queen from France and the marriage had actually taken place there, in secret and in haste, to escape the diplomatic pressure being put on the young widow by the French. When they arrived at Greenwich, faced by the fact that a commoner had married the king's sister without the royal consent, in the words of A. F. Pollard, Brandon 'saw the executioner's axe gleam before his eyes, and he trembled'. But Henry seems to have rejoiced in their happiness, and from then on Brandon and the

Queen-Dowager of France were the constant companions of the king and queen at Placentia.

Further great celebrations were arranged in May 1516 when Henry's other sister, Margaret, now Queen-Dowager of Scotland, visited her brother and his wife at Greenwich. Challenges were again issued to all comers by the king, Brandon, Essex, and the dashing young Master of Horse, Sir Nicholas Carew. Obviously by now there was a form to these occasions—the king, sometimes with one or two chosen companions, challenging every willing opponent to a show of strength. In 1524, during a visit of the Scots ambassadors, a castle, twenty feet square, fifty feet high and surrounded by a fifteen-foot ditch, was set up in the tilt-yard and joyfully assaulted. As usual, the king broke the most spears. England was at war with France at the time, and the Scots 'marvelled that the masks and revelry were continued . . . while their own country was saddened by war. The English assured the Scots that they did not value the French King a bean, for the people profited by war, and prayed for a continuance of it. Whereat the Scots much mused.'

The daytime pageantry was matched, indeed surpassed, by the revelry at night. Accounts of the entertainment show a fecund imagination and a carelessness about expenditure which must have left the rest of Europe gasping. To please his young queen, at Christmas 1511 Henry ordered a castle labelled *Le Fortresse Dangerus* to be erected in Greenwich's great hall. This he assaulted, dressed with five companions in russet satin and cloth of gold. Six ladies, similarly clothed, were within the castle; they were conquered and brought out, to dance before Catherine of Aragon, who clapped her hands with pleasure. In 1514 there was the same kind of entertainment, the costumes being of blue velvet and cloth of silver. At Christmas 1516 an artificial garden was laid in the great hall, and the ladies and gentlemen of the court danced in it, watched by the queens of England and Scotland.

In 1518 the French ambassador took barge to Greenwich, to

arrange a marriage between the king's two-year-old daughter, Mary, and the Dauphin, and the pageants perhaps exceeded anything that had gone before. Hall describes a tableau:

> A rock full of all manner of stones, with five trees on the top —an olive, a pine apple, a rose tree, a branch of lilies, and a pomegranate—bearing shields of the arms of Rome, the Emperor, England, France and Spain, as in league against the enemies of Christianity. On a rock sat a lady with a dolphin in her lap. Out of the rock came knights who fought at tourney, while a man mounted on a Pegasus expounded the meaning of the pastime, after which a banquet was served, of 260 dishes. This night the cupboard in the hall was of twelve stages, all of plate of gold and no gilt plate.

The emperor represented in this masque was Charles V, nephew of Catherine of Aragon. On a visit to Greenwich in 1522 he was 'lodged in the king's lodging, which was so richly hanged that the Spaniards wondered at it, and especially at the rich cloth of estate'. He brought a tremendous retinue with him, too large to be all housed in Placentia. A contemporary list of the available accommodation is wonderfully illuminating on the state of Greenwich at that time. 'My lord of Kentes howse, Master Carewes howse, Master Garnyshe howse, Master Noris howse' all took an unspecified number of the visitors, but nothing like *enough*. A canvass had to be made in the town to assess the amount of public and private accommodation offered; the former, it was found, could take in 360; the latter was able to provide a total of 129 beds (including eight featherbeds from William Cornyshe, Master of the King's Chapel) and private stabling for eighty-eight horses.

The following year, after a rainy day's jousting during which nevertheless more than three hundred lances were broken in under two and a half hours, an elaborate banqueting house was erected. The accounts describe many curious pieces of decoration invented for it, including lions, dragons, greyhounds all fashioned as candlesticks; a whole series of ornaments made from cast lead, including roses and 'castles'—perhaps the Tudor shorthand for these, which we understand as portcullises; buckram, gilt and painted for a mock ceiling; 'arches, a portal, fountain and arbor', also painted and gilded; and a profusion of plaster and paper adornments. This temporary building was put up in the tilt-yard.

There are some personal items in the accounts: 'garnishing a head piece with crown gold; making whistles, chains and aquilettes'. These were probably props for the performers in the evening's entertainment, but whether such people were profess-ional players and troubadours, or Henry and his guests, we do not know. That the dressing up of king and court was a major part of its function we can glean from all the chroniclers. Hall gives a bizarre anecdote about a pageant in the park which got out of hand, when the king allowed the people of Greenwich to approach so near that they started to tear at his clothes, and indeed stripped him

> into his hosen and doublet, and all his companions likewise. Syr Thomas Knevet stood on a stage and for all his defence he lost his apparel. The ladies likewise were spoyled. Wherefore the Kynges guard came suddenly, and put the people back. But a shipman of London caught certain letters ... H and K [for Henry and Katharine] made of fine gold to adorn the ladies' dresses; in every void place were spangles of gold, and every person had his name in like letters of massy gold ... which he sold to a goldsmith for iii £ xiiii s viii d.

But of course these were only the trappings of a success story. Henry VIII was the first monarch for nearly a hundred years who had not had to fight his fellow-countrymen for possession of his throne. The reign was a good one, and needed to be seen to be; beautiful, famous Greenwich was the perfect setting. Here, before his pale young queen, waited on by other queens, never taking part, always either pregnant or recovering from a miscarriage, was the might and panoply of England lovingly portrayed. Here she sat, clapped her thin little hands, laughed fondly at her husband and thanked him with kisses. If Henry occasionally overplayed his role of Prince Charming into Court Fool, did it matter? He was also doing more serious things, like building up the navy at the dockyards of Woolwich and Deptford; setting up a magnificent armoury; looking to foreign diplomacies; making a popular but not ruinous show of strength against France; encouraging with a rare sense of prudence and propriety the power of the church. 'Love for the King,' wrote a Venetian visitor to Greenwich about 1515, 'is universal with all who see him, for his Highness does not seem a person of this world, but one descended from heaven.'

Another Italian, the diplomat Agostino Guistiniani, wrote to Erasmus:

He is extremely handsome. Nature could not have done more for him. He is much handsomer than any other sovereign in Christendom, a great deal handsomer than the King of France.... He is very accomplished, a good musician, composes well; is a capital horseman, very fond of hunting, and never takes his diversion without tiring eight or ten horses—before he gets home they are all exhausted. He is extremely fond of tennis, at which game it is the prettiest thing in the world to see him play, his fair skin glowing through a shirt of the finest texture.

Erasmus had already met Henry as a boy in 1499, when he had walked over to Greenwich with Thomas More from the house of his friend William Blount, Lord Mountjoy, at Charlton. This same Mountjoy wrote to Erasmus on Henry's accession: 'Our King does not desire gold or gems or precious metals, but virtue, glory, immortality.' It is to the papal envoy, Chieregati, that we owe several descriptions of Henry's dress: 'White damask in the Turkish fashion, the robe all embroidered with roses made of rubies and diamonds'; 'royal robes down to the ground, of gold brocade lined with ermine'—the whole court, as Chieregati put it, 'glittering with jewels and gold and silver, the pomp being unprecedented'.

Adjoining Placentia on its western side was a house of Observant Friars; this was a branch of the Franciscan Order, established about 1415 but not represented in England until, in the year 1481, Edward IV had obtained permission from Pope Sixtus IV for a foundation at Greenwich. He had given the friars a piece of land next door to the palace, some twelve virgates by sixty-three virgates, 'where the game of ball used to be played', and had bought for them some old buildings near by. On 14 December 1485 Henry VII had confirmed his father-in-law's grant 'for a church, cemetery, cloister, refectory, dormitory, "ortos", and other premises', and set up a convent consisting of a warden and twelve brothers.

With his wife, Elizabeth of York, he had made frequent generous gifts to them; and his will had stated that they were to have £200 to enclose their garden and orchard with a brick wall, and a further £200 on trust for their use, as he 'knew they had been many times in peril of ruin for lack of food'. Henry VIII continued this affectionate and generous relationship. In 1513 he wrote to Pope Leo X saying he could not praise highly enough their 'strict adherence to poverty, their sincerity, charity and devotion. No Order battles more assiduously against vice, and none are more active in keeping Christ's fold.'

The poor, meek Observants, huddled in the shadow of the fabulous Placentia, may well have seemed a necessary corrective in local eyes; very many ordinary citizens of Greenwich contributed money or goods to the friars in what was obviously a spirit of affectionate gratitude. Thomas Ustwayte, builder of the mansion later occupied by the Earl of Worcester, left among other bequests '3s 4d for a light in the Chapel'; his will was witnessed by that other riverside mansion-builder, John Gunthorpe. Richard Carpenter, 'servant of the king, yeoman of the pantry', left 10s to the friars (to his son John, 'butler of the king's chamber', he left a satin coat). In 1524 John Stile, 'armourer to the King's Grace', left the friars 28s 6d. Alice Newman, whose will is specially interesting for the descriptions of silver it contains—she left, among other pieces, six apostle spoons with gilt knops to her daughter Agnes—bequeathed 10s to the friars. John Rolfe, whose ancestor had followed Duke Humphrey to Agincourt, left 10s for a trental of masses, while Agnes Newark, daughter-in-law of a Cade rebel, left a similar amount for a trental of sermons. Thomazine Sheby bequeathed the friars a diaper towel, twelve yards long, for use as an altar frontal; like many of the others, Thomazine also made benefactions to the parish church of St Alfege, among them a standing cup of silver gilt, 'under this condition, that every bride that shall be married in the church of St Alfege shall have the said cup borne before them at their marriage' if they so desired. The vicar of Greenwich himself, William Derlyngton, left 30s to the friars.

So the battle which broke out in the late 1520s between Henry VIII and the Church would have a particular meaning for the people of Greenwich. Catherine of Aragon is said to have belonged to the Third (lay) Order of St Francis, although it is difficult to see how, since one of the Order's rules demanded the wearing of clothes of an unobtrusive colour, and another forbade attendance at fêtes, balls and dancing parties. But she was certainly a constant and devout worshipper at the friars' church, very often slipping out of the palace at midnight to be present at the first sung service of the day; she expressed a wish to be buried in the convent, and appointed John Forrest (probably the warden) to be her confessor.

Queen Catherine of Aragon bore her husband four sons, perhaps five: her last child, its sex ignored by the historians, was born dead in 1518. But it was not until 1525, when she was forty years old, that Henry finally gave up hope of having an heir by her, and began to investigate the possibility of getting legitimate issue by someone else. Not unnaturally, the Observant Friars stood by their queen. Relations with the king began to grow strained. On Easter Sunday, 1532, the friars' provincial, William Peto, preached before Henry at Greenwich and warned him in plain terms that attempts to annul the marriage would endanger his crown. The rebuke seemed to be taken, Henry rising and stalking out in silence. But Cromwell sought and found spies among the friars, and from then on all the doings of the Observants were faithfully reported to the king's ministers.

In May 1533, shortly before the coronation of Anne Boleyn, William Peto again preached to the king about sin in high places. This time Henry ordered one of his chaplains, Dr Curwen, to answer the accusations in a sermon delivered in the same place the following Sunday. Curwen obliged, but one of the friars, the warden, Henry Elston, rebutted his words from the rood loft —to the king's great discomfiture, according to Stow. Henry had Elston and Peto arrested; but they managed to escape and fled to Antwerp. Others bravely took up the fight on Catherine's behalf. William Robinson preached for the queen at Paul's Cross in London; and Thomas Pearson was so bold as to rebuke the king's chaplain for speaking against her virtue. Two friars were caught in the act of sending letters to 'the princess dowager' as she must now be called. 'They would confess some great matter,' wrote Cromwell privately to the king, 'if they might be examined as they ought to be, that is to say by pains.' But the warden at Greenwich, now William Sydenham, managed to retain the punishment of them in his own hands; one of them, Hugh Payne, escaped to the west of England, where he went round publicly condemning the king's actions and preaching obedience to the Pope.

Once safely married to Anne Boleyn, Henry tried a different

tactic. He made lavish presents of alms to the Friars Observants, and arranged to have Princess Elizabeth christened in their church in an elaborate ceremony on 10 September 1533. By the end of the year a pardon had been arranged and granted. But there was to be a further demand for submission; on 13 April 1534 a royal commission was issued, compelling every friar to acknowledge on oath the king's position as supreme head of the Church, and six weeks later Henry's agents arrived at Greenwich ready to extract a mass oath from the Observants. The friars announced that they would 'answer particularly every man for himself'. Examined individually, each refused to accept the articles, especially that which denied the authority of the Pope. 'They had professed St Francis's religion,' they declared, 'and in the observance thereof they would live and die.'

Two days later, some cart-loads of friars were seen entering the Tower of London; it was not known where they were from. By the beginning of August the people of Greenwich realised their friars were gone. All had been taken into custody, some placed in prisons, some incarcerated in other monasteries. Rumours of terrible treatment soon reached back to Greenwich; but neither then nor ever later could they be accurately probed. It is certain that within a short time of their being taken into custody some thirty of the Greenwich friars were dead; what happened to the rest of them is not known. A very few have their method of dying recorded; Thomas Belcham, a young friar, a native of Greenwich, who had filled a book with the king's misdeeds, died of starvation in Newgate; so did Thomas Court. An unnamed friar, perhaps Anthony Brockby, after twenty-five days of torture which failed to kill him, was strangled with the cord of his habit.

After several months the oath of submission was again put to the brothers, and some took it; of these, a few were allowed to escape abroad. But of those refusing, Hugh Payne died in the Marshalsea in 1537; Anthony Browne, who fled from Greenwich before the closure, and had become a hermit, was arrested at Norwich in 1538, and tortured in the Tower for ten days before being executed. John Forrest, Catherine's confessor, had been imprisoned in the Grey Friars, London. Worn down by privation, he weakened and made a submission (telling his confessor he had denied the Pope by an oath given by the outward man but not the inward one), and was allowed some privileges. His confessor, Friar Wafferer, was a Cromwell spy: Forrest was seized and cast into Newgate, and on 22 May 1538, according to Hall's *Chronicles*, he was 'roasted alive as a traitor and heretic'.

Cruelly underlining these martyrdoms, Henry VIII bestowed a generous annuity on those Grey Friars who had acted as gaolers to the Observants, and in 1537 installed them in the empty convent at Greenwich. But by 1540 they too had gone and the friary was being used as a carpenter's shop.

Anne Boleyn was not beautiful, and it puzzled many people at the court to see what Henry VIII found in her. She was, went a report to the Venetians, 'of middling stature, swarthy complexion, long neck, wide mouth, bosom not much raised, and in fact has nothing but the King's great appetite, and her eyes, which are black and beautiful'. She had a malformation of one of her fingers which some people considered the brand sign of a witch; but there were many others, particularly those Greenwich citizens who had lived through the twenty years of Catherine's honourable reign and experienced the modest piety of the friars, who regarded her soberly as nothing more than a whore.

For Henry, of course, it was a joyful new beginning. He marked his happiness by having the palace redecorated; and building accounts give a vivid idea of the excitement underlying the preparations for receiving the mother of his heir. James Nedam was the king's surveyor-general, and his books record in detail the reglazing, retiling, repanelling and repaving that went on. The kitchens were extended, and several new windows were put in the royal apartments. In the king's privy chamber sixty-seven ceiling bosses were ordered, 'redy turned and carved for the fret', together with two hundred and eighteen buds and their accompanying leaves, 'all gilded and set upon two hundred and sixty-four yards of battens painted white'. Shelves were put up and trestle tables assembled; John Harrison of London, broderer, was paid 18s 8d for re-covering the king's stool with scarlet velvet and gilt nails. Even the armourers were taken off their work to make pieces for my Lady Anne Rochford; Erasmus Kyrkener, Master Armourer, 'garnished and gilded' some books for Anne, and made her a desk which he ornamented with 'latens and gold'.

Anne's coronation had been at Westminster; so the christening of her child was the first Greenwich ceremony at which she could parade herself as queen. An attempt was made to have the service as lavish as the christening of Mary, Catherine's daughter, had been. Once again the way between the palace and the church was railed and hung with arras (the men working all night by candlelight to finish it), and the entry furbished with needlework panels sewn with precious stones and pearls. Before the birth, while a son was still hoped for, Anne Boleyn had been so concerned to make the occasion grand that she had prevailed on Henry to ask Catherine of Aragon to lend the rich Spanish shawl which had wrapped Mary and Henry's sickly sons at the previous christenings. 'The Queen has replied,' wrote Eustace Chapuys to his master, Charles V, 'that it has not pleased God that she should.'

In spite of the lack of the shawl and the smouldering dispute with the friars, Elizabeth's christening was splendid. Her name was that of her grandmother, Elizabeth of York—still in many hearts secretly enthroned as Queen Regnant rather than Queen Consort. The godparents were Margaret, Marchioness of Dorset, the Dowager Duchess of Norfolk and Thomas Cranmer, Archbishop of Canterbury. A silver font had been placed on a platform in the middle of the church, covered with a fine cloth.

'Divers gentlemen with aprons,' wrote Edward Hall, 'and towels about their necks, gave attendance about it. That no filth should come into the Font, over it hung a square canopy of Crimson Satin fringed with gold.' Afterwards the mayor and aldermen of the city of London were taken to the palace cellar for a drink before departing in their barges.

Anne's queening at Greenwich lasted three neurotic years; with what many saw as divine justice, her stillborn son was born on the day that Catherine of Aragon went to her tomb. In the treason trial that almost automatically followed, her lovers were listed as Sir Francis Weston, Sir Henry Norris, Sir William Brereton and Mark Smeaton—the last-named being a groom of the chamber and a musician, a 'player on the espinette'. Henry VIII possessed twenty-two virginals, and a note in the accounts states that in May 1530 a pair of them, 'in one coffer wt iiij stoppes', was delivered to Greenwich.

Sir Henry Norris and Sir Francis Weston were both well known locally. Westons had held land in Lewisham of the abbot of Ghent under John Norbury and Henry Vannere, and a Thomas Weston had followed Humphrey of Gloucester to Agincourt. Sir Henry Norris was steward of the manor of Greenwich; it was to his house in the town that the king's peacocks had been removed in 1534 'because the Queen's Grace could not take her rest in the mornings for the noise of the same'.

It need not surprise us that these men should be arraigned as the paramours of Anne Boleyn. They would be familiar figures about the court, known to all, but minor personalities, unprotected by great wealth or noble birth. Guilty or not guilty, Anne's loud and egotistical behaviour had not endeared her to the king's subjects. Bad manners and bad morals were obverse and reverse of the same coin—or so might have said many of the people of Greenwich as they lined the banks of the Thames to see 'the Concubine' taken to the Tower. They watched in silence as she went; and there is no doubt that the vast majority were glad to see her go. Among those who were to provide evidence for Cromwell's dossier was Mrs Cosyn, member of a Greenwich family who had been royal servants at the palace of Placentia for several generations. Agneys Cosyn had looked after the bed linen for Elizabeth of York. Her grand-daughter 'lay on the Queen's pallet' and faithfully reported to the Constable of the Tower everything the distraught creature said.

Anne Boleyn

CHAPTER 8

Inheritors of Henry VIII

There is a temptation at Greenwich to dismiss the three reigns that intervened between Henry VIII and his brilliant daughter. The king in the codpiece: the virgin queen—they complement each other too well to be parted. In fact, Elizabeth's reign was separated from her father's by eleven years of considerable confusion; and there had been a full decade of uneasiness even before. Greenwich could never have been a comfortable place after Catherine of Aragon's death. In spite of all the pseudo-gaiety, sexual excitements, self-conscious struttings of the succeeding wives, the pageantry had lost its meaning. In all such contrived displays there has to be somewhere a virtue, a sincerity. It was this that Catherine had provided.

Not every moment was tense, of course; the household accounts give small gleams of domestic contentment, as when the two daughters, Mary and Elizabeth, both temporarily forgiven for their mothers, provide their father with a consort of minstrels, and share the expense between them; receive a present of cherries from the nearby garden of Lady Garnish; watch while the newest stepmother, Anne of Cleves, picks her amiable way over the brow of the park, along a path specially cut for her through the thorns. But Greenwich could not be other than a haunted place, and the court gradually moved away to Hampton.

Edward VI's reign has one particular importance for Greenwich; just as Humphrey of Gloucester may be said to be the instigator of its present geography, so Edward laid the foundation for the present land tenure. His actions arose naturally from those of his father, for Henry VIII by his dissolution of the monasteries had broken at last the ecclesiastical hold on Greenwich first placed there by Elstrudis in 918. In Henry's time those parts of the manor not enclosed within the Placentia fence and not given privately elsewhere had been awarded for his life to the courtier Sir Richard Long. At Long's death these lands, under the name of Old Court, became ripe for plucking.

Among Edward VI's courtiers was John Dudley, whose father, Edmund Dudley, had been executed at the very outset of Henry VIII's reign. As a boy of eight young John Dudley had been adopted by Sir Edward Guilford, Master of the King's Armoury, and in 1520 he married Sir Edward's daughter, Jane. The alliance brought him powerful local connections, including the Hautes; and it must have taught him, too, the historic value of the Greenwich manor. It did not take him long to acquire a complete ascendancy over the king. In 1550, shortly after he had been created Earl of Warwick and Viscount Lisle, Dudley arranged with the thirteen-year-old Edward to have Old Court transferred to himself. An indenture of the properties, dated 18 July 1550, lists: 'The capital mansion house with appurtenances near the Queen's stables, by the Thames, at the East end of E. Greenwich . . . and the three stables called the Queen's stables, and a barn there, at the East end of the said mansion. Also the reversion of the lordship or manor of Old Court (80 acres of mead, 20 acres upland, 80 acres marsh) with the tithes of fruit, hay and corn in E. and W. Greenwich to this said manor belonging.'

There was a local girl in the royal circle, daughter of the lord of the manor of Lee. This was Lady Jane Grey. Her father, Henry Grey, Marquis of Dorset, had married Frances, child of the romantic union between Mary, Queen-Dowager of France, and Charles Brandon, Duke of Suffolk; and this lineage made Jane a possible heiress to the Tudor throne. It was not a situation to be neglected; and when in the spring of 1553 it became obvious to John Dudley, now Duke of Northumberland, that the boy king was mortally ill, he arranged a marriage between Lady Jane Grey and his own son, Lord Guilford Dudley.

They must have been grim times at Placentia. To refute stories that Edward was already dead, Dudley had the ashen, shaking boy propped up at a window where the people of Greenwich could see him as they walked beside the river. He also got him to write out a 'devise for the succession' which named Jane as heir to the throne. The last weeks of Edward's life are wracked with rumour. For many years afterwards it was openly said that he had been poisoned. Yet without doubt his death from natural causes was imminent.

About the middle of June, the royal physicians told Northumberland that Edward must die within three days. One explanation of subsequent events is that it was necessary for the fructification of Dudley's plans that Henry VIII's other two children, Mary and Elizabeth, must be in his hands at the moment of the king's death, and that the doctors' notice was too short. Accordingly, the boy's own attendants were dismissed. He was moved out of Placentia into Dudley's Old Court property east of the palace, and a female quack installed who stopped Edward's consumptive haemorrhages by administering arsenic. Three weeks were thus added to his life; and when poor Edward, in great agony from the poison, with hair all fallen out and gangrenous fingers and toes, finally breathed his last on 6 July, the plans for Jane's accession were as ready as they could be.

But what to do with the body? There could be no lying-in-state and no embalming. Even to glimpse the corpse would be to guess at some frightful malpractice. When the lord mayor and sheriffs of London were summoned to Greenwich on the afternoon of 7 July, they were only told of the death of their young sovereign, and not shown his remains. A letter from an exiled Catholic, John Burcher, hints that the duke 'had buried him privately in a paddock adjoining the palace, and substituted in his place, to be seen by the people, a young man not very unlike him, whom they had murdered'. Hester Chapman, biographer of Lady Jane Grey, wonders whether 'the bones now lying beneath the altar of the Chapel of Henry VII in Westminster Abbey are not Edward VI's, and that his dust has been disseminated in the suburbs of Greenwich . . .' and a small reinforcement of this gruesome idea may be found in a report (by Thomas Fuller in *Holy State*) that after Edward's funeral, and before Northumberland had been brought to execution on Tower Hill on 24 August, a boy's voice had been heard calling from beneath the altar in the Henry VII Chapel, crying out for vengeance. People naturally assumed the ghostly cries to belong to Edward. But might not this have been the murdered substitute, drawing attention by spectral means to his own dreadful fate?

In fact, Mary's succession was inevitable; looking back, one can only marvel at the capacity shown by John Dudley for self-deception. She was now thirty-eight, the undoubted daughter of Henry VIII. Many Greenwich people must have remembered her christening at the friars' church in 1516, and an early act of her reign was to reinstate the brethren there. William Peto, who had so bravely championed her mother, was called back to office; so was that other survivor of the holocaust, the courageous Henry Elston. But something had happened to England in the interim. There was no tolerance now for friars in Greenwich, and in July 1555 Peto and Elston had cause to complain to the queen that 'on Sunday last' as they passed into Greenwich from London, they were 'beaten with stones which were flung at us by divers lewd persons'. Dislike had turned to hatred by the following March, when the same friars' church saw the consecration of Cardinal Pole as Archbishop of Canterbury, only two days after the burning of Cranmer.

There were other unhappinesses; under Sir Henry Jerningham, the new steward, no game was to be taken within ten miles

of Greenwich Park. His predecessor in the stewardship—by a
deed drawn up at Greenwich on the last day but one of poor
Edward's life—had been the local worthy, Sir John Gates. With
another local man, Sir Thomas Palmer (owner of extensive
marshland in north Woolwich, besides farms and orchards in
Mottingham and Lee), Gates rose and fell with the Duke of
Northumberland, and paid the same penalty. Meeting Dudley on
Tower Hill on the day when both were executed, he was just
able to exchange the platitudes appropriate to the occasion, but
unable to forgive. Palmer's bearing on the scaffold was exemp-
lary. His farewell speech—'I have seen death and know how
little it is to be feared'—was quoted approvingly by that con-
noisseur of such occasions, Holinshed.

Of the Greys, Thomas, Jane's uncle, and Henry, her father,
both went to their execution in the spring of 1554. Much of
their Lee estates later passed to the Hatcliffes. As for John
Dudley's five handsome sons by Jane Guilford, Lord Guilford
Dudley died with his wife Jane Grey on the scaffold. John and
Henry were both dead by 1555. Ambrose, who succeeded his
elder brother as Earl of Warwick, did his best to recoup the
family's honour with a long and loyal service to Elizabeth, dying
in 1599. But it was Robert Dudley, created Earl of Leicester in
1564, who caught the English romantic imagination—because he
caught the fancy of the queen.

Robert Dudley's long but spasmodic courtship of Elizabeth
steps its slow way across the courts of Placentia like the figuring
of a pavanne. Whether he and his fellow suitors really thought
it likely that they would acquire the sovereign as wife is unlikely
ever to be known. His earldom had been bestowed on him in
the expectation that he would marry Mary, Queen of Scots; but
in the event Elizabeth could not bring herself to send him north.
In *Kenilworth* Sir Walter Scott makes Dudley's first marriage,
to Amy Robsart, the subject of scandal, royal displeasure and
eventual murder. But the Robsart marriage was the one that

Elizabeth must have known about—it had taken place in 1550 when Dudley was a boy of seventeen.

A cause of much greater danger to his career was the intrigue with the curiously named Douglas, wife of Lord Sheffield. Historians place the clandestine association of these two—which resulted in the birth of Dudley's only surviving son—at Esher; but at least in its early stages a much more likely place was Greenwich, where both of them must be because of court duties, and where Leicester's house stood in its acre of gardens south of the present pier, separated from the palace by the Friars' Road and a high brick wall. Long after Leicester's death, giving evidence before a court of the Star Chamber on 10 May 1605, Douglas described the circumstances of her parting from him, at an assignation arranged with great discretion in the close arbour of the queen's garden at Placentia, where he told her in the presence of Sir John Hubbard and George Digby that their liaison was at an end.

The reason for the break was his wish to marry another local young woman, Lettice Knollys, daughter of Sir Francis Knollys of Lewisham, and granddaughter of that earlier charmer, Mary Boleyn. Marriage may not have been in his mind; but warned by poor Douglas's fate, Sir Francis insisted, and the nuptials took place at Wanstead in 1578, in the presence of his brother Ambrose, the bride's father, and members of the court, the only important absentee being the queen herself. It was this marriage that the French diplomat, Jean de Simier, revealed to Elizabeth, perhaps as a revenge for a shooting incident, also in the queen's garden at Greenwich, when a member of her guard had fired on him—as he believed, at the instigation of Leicester.

Elizabeth's grief and rage were all the greater for the manner of the revelation; and Robert Dudley was ordered to the Tower. The Earl of Sussex was the tactful courtier who suggested that the punishment would be equally severe and the monarch's dignity better served if the Tower at Greenwich were substituted

—that ancient tower now named Mireflore and acquiring Tudor legend of its own as the fortress where her father had housed more than one of his own secret infatuations.

A fascinating survival exists of these days, recorded in the painting now at Penshurst (page 68), traditionally known as *Queen Elizabeth Dancing with Robert Dudley, Earl of Leicester.* The picture is one of a series, all depicting marriages of members of the French court; and it seems to be a piece of political wishful-thinking concerned with the hurrying on of Elizabeth's projected wedding to Henri III's younger brother, the Duc d'Alençon. As in the French paintings, which are of known occasions, set recognisably in the Louvre, one may at least tentatively identify many of the figures shown. Elizabeth's partner would appear to be—as accepted in Lord De L'Isle's family tradition—Robert Dudley himself. The two young women in dark gown and open-necked ruff are wearing the dress of her maids of honour. D'Alençon, for whom the party was given, may be equated with the slightly frog-like young man in pale-coloured doublet and hose and plumed brown hat, sitting with his back to us on the right of the scene.

Perhaps most interesting to the Greenwich historian are the musicians. We know so much about Elizabeth's Greenwich players—and here they are: Alfonso Ferrabosco, playing the instrument in which he specialised, the bass viol; behind him the two 'treble viols' (violins), his fellow-countryman, Galliardello, and the English Richard Farrant; with, on the extreme left of the group, the young John Lanier, his sabeca strapped on a harness round his shoulders.

But although Robert Dudley holds the romantic stage, probably the young Edward Courtenay, son of Henry Courtenay, Earl of Devon, late of the Swanne House, of all Elizabeth's suitors may claim to have put the most historic stamp on Greenwich. Edward's grandmother had been Katherine, daughter of Edward IV and Elizabeth Widville; he was spoken of as 'the last sprig of the White Rose' and treated with a royal deference. It was he who Mary's council would have wished her to marry, in preference to the hated Philip of Spain; and he was also seen as a suitable husband for Elizabeth. But Edward's youth had been spent as a prisoner in the Tower, where he had been taken with his mother at his father's execution; and after fifteen incarcerated years he had so flaunted his freedom in loose living as to become unacceptable as a bridegroom to either of Henry VIII's daughters.

The Courtenay roots were in Devon; and following the family to Greenwich had come a long procession of Devonians. It may well have been a return home for some of the blood in their veins; as long ago as the Conquest, when William of Normandy had selected Walter of Douai as a Greenwich defender, there had been a traffic between this part of the Thames and the Douai holdings in Devon. Drake's *Hundred of Blackheath* gives a list of surnames common to both places in the fourteenth century; they included Calvel, Amis, Spicer, Joliffe, Mayhew, Kemp, Bedick and Chapman. The last name is of great interest to local historians; the Chapman family were seamen in Devon, shipwrights at Greenwich, from the reign of Edward I if not before. By Elizabeth's time Richard Chapman, described as owner of a private shipyard at Deptford, had the title Queen's Master Shipwright and the task of building river defences along the Thames, together with Peter Pett and Mathew Baker. (His son, Edmund Chapman, Chief Joiner to the Queen, has already been noted as the buyer of the Swanne House—significantly when one remembers its connection with the Courtenays. Possibly he was holding it until the attainder could be reversed; certainly Edward Courtenay was back, living at Greenwich during the reign of Edward VI.)

For more than a decade Europe had watched while the mighty Spaniards martialled their forces, and their defiant little victim crouched behind her sea frontier. The year before his death

Henry VIII had instituted the Navy Board, and in the 1560s and 1570s tremendous efforts were made by the men who served on it to put the English fleet in a state fit to meet the power of Spain. This meant, as every student of naval history is taught, changing the idea that a battleship was no more than a floating castle, and making it a fast, flexible weapon in its own idiom. The men who were responsible for this new thought in sea warfare, and all the long-drawn-out reorganisation that must accompany it, were centred at West Greenwich (or Deptford): chief among them was the Treasurer of Marine Causes, John Hawkins.

But this was the last chapter in Spanish matters, not the first. For that we must go back to January 1554, and the announcement that Queen Mary Tudor and Philip of Spain were to be married. It was an intolerable proposition for many Englishmen, among them Edward Courtenay and Sir Thomas Wyatt (?1521–54). The latter, son of a poet-courtier of Henry VIII, was of mixed Devon and Kent connections. He owned Alington Castle and had married in 1537 yet another Jane Haute—this one the daughter of Sir William Haute of Bishopsbourne. Mary's Spanish marriage was to have been the signal to spark off a great all-England rebellion; but in the event only Wyatt managed to do anything effective. He made a proclamation at Maidstone, set up rebel headquarters at Rochester, collected 4,000 men and marched through Dartford and Gravesend to Blackheath, where he camped on 29 January 1554. He then found, like so many of his predecessors, that London was impregnable, lost his supporters' confidence, surrendered and was executed on 11 April. The story has all the familiar sad features about it.

In one aspect, however, it differs from the earlier rebellions. The impetuous Wyatt rose, as so many of his kind have done, too early. Wyatt's hatred of Spain, though—to be shared some thirty years later by every right-minded Englishman—sparked off a train of effort which, by bringing together the two weapons that only conjoined could annihilate Spanish sea power, was to save England. Without him, it is more than likely that either the brave men or the handy ships they sailed would not have been there together in 1588 to complement each other.

The war with Spain was, of course, a religious war; English anti-Spaniards were fighting the cause of Protestantism. Yet, as Dr Drake, chief editor of Hasted's *Hundred of Blackheath*, points out, historians have paid singularly little attention to the fact that Devon seamen and their families were championing this same cause in a profoundly important collaboration with those Greenwich Protestants who had been such close witnesses of Henry VIII's schism with Rome. Dr Drake names the heads of the anti-Spain party of 1554 (the men who were behind Sir Thomas Wyatt's rebellion) as Sir Gawen Carew and Sir Peter Carew, son and grandson of Henry VIII's jousting companion and Master of Horse, Sir Nicholas; Sir Arthur Champernown, Sir James Crofts and Henry Grey, Duke of Suffolk, father of Lady Jane. He adds:

Too little importance has been attached to the fact that, like Courtenay, Princess Elizabeth was of Devonshire extraction. Yet, it is of moment in a perilous conspiracy that the chiefs should be knitted together by relationship or a common religion or some tie stronger than a political one as their guarantee against treachery.

Historians are silent on the earlier connections of the Carews with the Reformation. Kat Ashley, the Princess Elizabeth's governess, when under examination on 24 February 1549, confessed that at Slanning's house in London she met Lady Barkley, aunt of Edward Courtenay; Lady Denny, niece of Sir Gawen Carew, sister of Sir Arthur Champernown, and sister-in-law of Lady Barkley; the brothers Archdeacon Carew and Sir Gawen Carew, with their nephew Sir Peter Carew; Thomas Parry, the Princess's cofferer, whose wife, Lady Anne Fortescue, was in tribulation lest her husband should be arrested.

John Slanning was the grantee of Skinner's Place in Deptford (which later passed to Elizabeth's Lord High Admiral, Lord Howard), and of Bickley in Devon, which adjoined the seat of Sir Francis Drake. His nephew, Nicholas Slanning, married the granddaughter of Lady Champernown. Thomas Parry was the grandson of Sir Thomas Vaughan, who was executed by Richard III at Pontefract in 1483 with Earl Rivers, Lord Richard Grey and Sir Richard Haute.

Lady Denny was one of the court ladies whom the noble-spirited Anne Askew, put on the rack at Greenwich after an examination there lasting five hours, had refused to betray. Her nieces were by marriage also the nieces of Sir Peter Carew; her nephew, Sir Gawen Champernown, was Sir Francis Drake's friend and companion. Her brave sister Catherine was the mother of Raleigh.

Lady Anne Parry's former husband, Sir Adrian Fortescue, was Anne Boleyn's cousin, which fact may account for the grant of Charlton to her by Queen Elizabeth. The Carews were also related to Anne Boleyn, her ancestor Sir Geoffrey Boleyn and Sir James Carew having married sisters. Brought up at Greenwich, old Sir Gawen Carew had married Anne Brandon, sister of Charles Brandon, brother-in-law of Henry VIII. His second wife was Mary, daughter of Sir Robert Wotton of Bocton, Kent, and widow of Sir Henry Guilford—great-uncle of Lord Guilford Dudley and uncle of Sir Thomas Wyatt's wife. Margaret, the sister of Mary Wotton, was mother of Henry Grey, Duke of Suffolk, and grandmother of Lady Jane Grey. The wife of his nephew, Sir Peter Carew, and the wife of Ambrose Dudley, Earl of Warwick, were sisters-in-law, and his nephew John Champernown was an uncle by marriage of young Edward Courtenay.

Dr Drake might have added many more of these Devon-

Greenwich links. Sir Thomas Wyatt's mother, Elizabeth Brooke, was a great-granddaughter of Sir Geoffrey Boleyn. Sir Peter Carew was brother-in-law of William Hatcliffe, whose grandfather had married the widow of Roger Fitz of Rushey Green Place, a house very near where the abbot of Ghent had his Lewisham priory. The Fitz family owned large estates at Tavistock, and Roger's nephew's wife, Agnes Grenville, was great-aunt of Sir Richard Grenville of the *Revenge*; his great-nephew's wife, Mary Sydenham, was aunt to Lady Francis Drake. Elizabeth Drake herself married as her second husband Sir William Courtenay, who acquired the Fitz estates at Lewisham and whose descendants were to inherit Edward Courtenay's earldom of Devon.

How all these ties between Devon families and the ancient manor of Greenwich originated is not clearly understood; but that they were sustained by sea traffic can scarcely be doubted. We know that ships of Devon and Cornwall, passing up Channel in the fourteenth century, incurred the wrath of the Cinque ports by failing to show proper respect—a striking of topsails—as they went by. In 1378 a Thames-bound fleet of Courtenay vessels had been overpowered in the Straits of Dover by Spanish raiders. Lord Audley's Cornish rebellion of 1497, indeed, had made for Blackheath in the hope of joining up with Devon and Cornwall sympathisers.

We may take a look at the early life of Francis Drake, that quintessentially Devon man, whose seamanship was undoubtedly learned on the waters of Thames and Medway. Drake's father, Edmund Drake, had fled from the farm at Crowndale, Tavistock, where he was born, at the Catholic rising of 1549. The family reached Plymouth and got passage in a ship bound for the Medway. This was the time when Deptford warships were overflowing into Gillingham Reach, and here was where young Francis Drake played as a child, the family living aboard one of the naval hulks. He must have heard his elders discussing Wyatt's rebellion, may even have seen something of the camp at Rochester.

He was apprenticed at the age of about twelve to the master of a small trading bark, 'coasting', according to the historian William Camden (1551–1623), 'along the shore and sometimes carrying merchandise into Zeeland and France'. This merchandise would assuredly have come over Thames wharves, and the young Drake must have grown very familiar with Greenwich. At his master's death the bark was left to him; and with the accession of Elizabeth and the restoration of the Protestant faith, the family fortunes revived in another direction, his father being made vicar of Upchurch, Kent. But with the new reign, too, war with Catholic Spain became inevitable.

At Deptford was Sir John Hawkins—not only a fellow Devonian but a kinsman. Drake sold his bark and joined the Hawkins fleet. At Deptford he came across Peter Pett, Mathew Baker, Richard Chapman, the men whose innovations in design and building techniques were to produce the ships that beat the Armada.

There must have been many Greenwich men helping both to build and to sail the British ships, but this was nothing new. In 1406 the king's vessel, the *Holigost*, had been given to John Mayhew of Greenwich and Fowey by Henry IV, 'in consideration of the loss Mayhew had suffered from French privateers'. Four ships 'of Greenwich' or 'king's ships' had fought in the French wars of 1512–14. Now at the new Medway base were ten 'queen's ships' late of Greenwich, with four attendant pinnaces and over 2,000 men on the pay list. There was also a squadron of smaller ships, crewed by 800 men, whose job was to stay behind and guard the Straits of Dover and the mouth of the Thames when the main fleet joined Drake at Plymouth. This squadron was under the command of Sir Henry Palmer, nephew of that Sir Thomas Palmer who had shared the scaffold with Gates and Dudley.

Incorporated with it was a land force of 2,000 men, sent to camp at Tilbury with the express duty of guarding the queen's person at Greenwich. The men of this very important force must have been selected specially for their local knowledge; of the nine colonels in charge, William and Francis Knollys were of the manor of Lewisham; Edmund Grey was of Lee; Sir William Halton held Greenwich property once owned by John Norbury; Sir Henry Goodyer was a connection of the Hautes; Sir John Smith owned thirty Greenwich houses and more than a thousand acres of Greenwich marsh.

The Armada sailed up the English Channel during the last ten days of July 1588. (It was said that every galleon carried a copy of Wyngaerde's drawings of Greenwich.) Once Calais Roads had been left behind, as we now know, the battle was over. Yet, as A. M. Hadfield has pointed out in *Time to Finish the Game*, the people of England were unable to realise for another six months or more that a great victory had been won. Not until the following November, when a sumptuous capture of Thomas Cavendish's from the Spanish Main was brought home and sailed up the Thames to Greenwich for the queen's inspection, did the triumph begin to seep in; it was 'a ship full of Spanish finery and treasure from Central America. It rained all day but the Queen went on board. Every sailor had a gold chain round his neck, the sails of the ship were of blue damask, and the standard was of cloth of gold and blue silk.'

So, after all, the war was not only religious; captures such as this, and the wider rivalries inherent in the quest for El Dorado, coloured the sixteenth-century mind. All over maritime Britain people were inspired by a dream of gold hitherto Spanish; but it was at Greenwich that the greatest sea knowledge and the richest patronage overlapped. Elizabeth herself became the largest shareholder in the voyages westward, summoning her captains to a farewell audience as they came downstream from Deptford, then waving at an open window of Placentia as they sailed away.

Frobisher was seen off in this manner on 7 June 1576, when he set out on his first quest for the North-West Passage. On his second, in 1577, Ambrose Dudley was there making his own farewells, since of the three ships, *Ayde, Gabriel* and *Michael,* he had provided the last two; the first was given by the queen.

Drake was received after his circumnavigation, 'with a finer banquet', reported the Spanish ambassador sourly, 'than has ever been seen in England since the time of King Henry'. It was served aboard the *Golden Hind* at Deptford; and Elizabeth, making a joke about striking off the head that had been demanded by the king of Spain, knighted Drake with a special gilded sword, in the presence of vast numbers of her subjects. The same sword was used again, in sight of another huge crowd, subjects of a second Elizabeth, when Francis Chichester was knighted on the Admiral's lawn at Greenwich in 1967.

Once begun, the impetus to explore was unending. To take as one example the voyage in search of the North-West Passage: Captain Waymouth, setting out from Deptford in 1602, was sponsored by 'the Worshipfull Fellowship of the Merchants of London trading into the East Indies'; seven of the ten-man committee appointed to equip the expedition were of Greenwich. Henry Hudson, who gave his name to Hudson's Bay, fitted out from here in 1610. Sir Thomas Button sailed under the patronage of the young Prince Henry of Wales in May 1612 (by the following November the young patron was dead, long before his new house at Charlton was ready for him). Bylot, Baffin, Luke Fox —all sailed down-Thames in search of the elusive north-west way to China, to scatter Greenwich names on the map of North America, with local men, local stores, local prayers going with them. Mostly the names were of their patrons or their shipmates; but there is a Charlton Island in Hudson's Bay, and a great bay on the south shore of Newfoundland called Placentia.

Queen Elizabeth ruled for forty-four years. She was sixty-nine when she died, and the young ministers of her youth had grown old with her. The court pageant evolving so exotically round the volatile Henry had stultified into a ritual which amazed foreign visitors. The German, Paul Hentzner, sailing down the Thames on a visit to Greenwich in 1598, noting as he passed Deptford the ship of 'that Noble Pirate, Sir Francis Drake' on show there, has left a long and detailed account of the ceremonial he found at Placentia.

We were admitted by order procured from the Lord Chamberlain, into the Presence Chamber, hung with rich tapestry . . . when it was time to go to prayers, the Queen came from her own apartment, attended in the following manner: First went Gentlemen, Barons, Earls, Knights of the Garter, all richly dressed and bare-headed; next came the Chancellor bearing the Seals in a red-silk purse, between two; one of which carried the Royal Scepter, the other the Sword of State, in a red scabbard, studded with golden Fleurs de Lis, the point upwards. Next came the Queen, in the sixty-fifth year of her age, as we were told, very majestic; her face oblong, fair, but wrinkled; her eyes small, yet black and pleasant; her nose a little hooked; her lips narrow, and her teeth black (a defect that the English seem subject to, for their too great use of sugar); she had in her ears two pearls, with very rich drops; she wore false hair, and that red; upon her head she had a small crown. . . . Her bosom was uncovered, as all the English ladies have it till they marry; and she had on a necklace of exceeding fine jewels; her hands were small, her fingers long, and her stature neither tall nor low; her air was stately, her manner of speaking mild and obliging.

That day she was dressed in white silk, bordered with pearls of the size of beans, and over it a mantle of black silk, shot with silver threads; her train was very long, the end of it borne by a marchioness; instead of a chain, she had an oblong collar of gold and jewels. As she went along in all this state and magnificence she spoke very graciously, first to one, then to another. . . . Whoever speaks to her, it is kneeling. Wherever she turned her face, as she was going along, everybody fell down on their knees.

In spite of the stilted court life, which she may well have enjoyed, Elizabeth moved freely among her subjects, walking daily in the park—'and outside it', as Rowland White reported to Sir Robert Sidney at Penshurst. She was fond of going along the waterfront, eastward past her own palace chapel, past the outlying buildings, to dine at Lumley House, on the site of the present Trinity Hospital. Both wives of Lord Lumley had been her friends; both had known Greenwich since their childhood.

Lord Lumley had found a picture of Richard II nailed on a basement wall in his house, and had given it to the queen, perhaps on one of these visits to dinner. She described the discovery to the Kent historian, William Lambarde, when he came to see her one morning in 1601, and presented her with a copy of his *Account of the Records of the Tower*. But perhaps her greatest pleasure in visiting Lumley House lay in the recollection that this was where John Dudley, Duke of Northumberland, had brought up his five handsome sons—that from this house her Robin, in the days before he was married to anybody, had looked out on the river and dreamed his young dreams.

Elizabeth I in 1601

CHAPTER 9

Stuart Elegance

In spite of their preoccupation with procreation, the Tudors left no heir. On 24 March 1603 it was a Stuart from Scotland who succeeded to the English crown; and which found the new situation more foreign, king or people, it is hard to guess. Elizabeth's fantastic day-long ceremonial, with its ritual processions and dressings-up, was an impossible one for James I and VI to continue, even if he had wanted to. He was not castable into the Tudor mould, and although he thoroughly enjoyed his new status—'Blessed be God's gracious goodness, who hath brought me into the promised land'—his Greenwich stewardship was to be sensible, practical, dignified and—a strange quality to find in one classed so often as a buffoon—supremely elegant.

But first there was the taking over. In a typically facetious letter to his secretary, Sir Robert Cecil, written before an early visit to the palace in 1605, he wrote:

> If I find not at my coming that the big chamberlain have ordered well all my lodging, that the little saucy constable have made the house sweet and built a cockpit, and that the fast-walking keeper of the park have the park in good order and the does all in fawn . . . then shall I at my return make the fat chamberlain to puff, the little cankered beagle to whine and the tall, black and cat-faced keeper to glower.

Greenwich outside Placentia had suffered neglect during the last years of Elizabeth's reign, and soon after James's arrival a petition was sent to Cecil, to pass on to the new king, for the paving of the main streets which were described as 'loathsome, dangerous and infectious'. The parish church was in a state of 'great ruyne and deformitie' and the steeple above the cracked square tower was daily expected to fall. What happened about the pavements is not recorded. The steeple was found to be beyond repair, and the churchwarden, John Hulett, who was also a Gentleman of the King's Chamber, borrowed £200 and had it rebuilt, apparently expecting that his royal master would meet the bill. But he never did; in Charles I's reign they were still petitioning for reimbursement.

In Scotland, James had ruled in the way in which William the Conqueror and the Plantagenets had done—as the most powerful lord in a glittering circle of near-equals. After the Wars of the Roses the Tudors had changed this style of monarchy in England, putting a psychological distance between themselves and the aristocracy. Logically enough, this was to produce a substantial change of building pattern in the places where they chose to live. In Greenwich the effect is clear; thirteenth- and fourteenth-century records show a smallish royal residence, with homes of almost equal grandeur, such as the Swanne House, studded round it. Henry VI's long minority brought about a dispersal of the nobility. It was the Tudor regrouping after the York–Lancaster holocaust that raised up a vast palace—the sun: with its planets, a circle of lesser though still large and ornate mansions clustering round it.

James's assumption of the English crown ended all that. It was not acceptable—perhaps not possible—for English noblemen to go back to the chief-among-equals style of kingship. Although of course they still attended court, from now on only the clerically-minded among them would jockey for state office; for all, the usual pattern of living would be to enjoy whatever country houses fitted congenially into their holdings of land, and to have a town house in London—not any longer within the city walls but along that other stretch of Thames, the Strand.

For Greenwich, the change was to be an immediate and disadvantageous one; with Courtenays gone, Dudleys gone, Greys gone, Comptons gone, the seventeenth-century scene begins to have a distinctly more homespun look. On several occasions during the Stuart regime the vestry, or parish council, had cause to complain to the tax-gatherers about the difficulties of administration with so many large houses now in multiple occupation.

There remained the Howards. The first documented connection of this great family with the district comes at the end of the fourteenth century, with Sir Robert Howard marrying Margery, daughter of Lord Scales, and so acquiring an estate at Woolwich. Sir John Howard, 1st Duke of Norfolk, was a Yorkist, prospering with Edward IV but supporting Richard III and dying with him on Bosworth Field. Fluctuating fortunes in Tudor times bring honours and executions in equal measure to many families; but at all Greenwich events of importance Howards are there. Anne Boleyn was through her mother a Howard; so, of course, was her cousin Queen Katherine. Their great-aunt, Lady Muriel Knyvett, dying in London in 1512, had been given an elaborate torchlight funeral procession down the Thames from Lambeth, and a lavish burial in the friars' church; she was the sister of Thomas Howard, Duke of Norfolk, and Thomas's duchess was to be godmother in the same church to each of Henry VIII's daughters. His son and his grandson were both beheaded, and he himself came near it in 1546 when he was attainted. It was his younger grandson, Henry—Henry Howard, Earl of Northampton, the man who with Cecil had done so much to prepare the new king for his heritage—who held the Howard possessions in Greenwich at the start of the Stuart dynasty.

On 11 October 1604 the manor of Old Court was given by James I to Sir Robert Cecil; Cecil promptly sold it to Henry Howard. (What he actually sold, it seems apparent from subsequent documents, was a 66-year lease.) Howard, who in his own words had been brought up 'from a child in the lodge in Greenwich Park', already had an obsessional love of the place. Now he lavished more than £2,000 on the buildings, put the land 'in good plight', and, according to Camden, 'much enlarged and beautified the Castle, in which he resided'. He bought the keepership of the park from Henry Lanman for £200, and seems to have had the intention of reuniting all Greenwich under one ownership (his own) as it had been in the days of the abbot of Ghent; two old Lee manors, 'the landes in Leigh Banckers and Shrofeilde purchased by me from his Majestie', are mentioned in his will. In 1605 he bought the house in its acre of ground to the west of the palace that had once belonged to Robert Dudley, Earl of Leicester, paying Robert's heir, his son by Douglas Sheffield (née Howard), £500 for it. For the same sum he acquired Lord Lumley's house at the latter's death in 1609.

But King James was out of sympathy with the idea of territorial lords and their possessions. In 1607 he had winkled out of Robert Cecil the great mansion at Theobalds; and on 25 November 1613 that indefatigable letter-writer John Chamberlain sent word to Sir Dudley Carleton in Venice that 'the Queen hath gained Greenwich into her Joynter.' The news horrified Henry Howard: 'The Queen says she will have the park in despight of me,' he wrote to a friend, 'although I bought it with my own money and have the same right as any other subject in the kingdom to his freehold.' He sent a letter to Sir Thomas Lake, the king's under-secretary, beseeching him to allow him to remain, and pointing out that 'it might be that her Majesty will not find a servant to keep with so much tenderness as I have done, the ground and the deer and the little wood that is left there.'

In spite of his pleas, on 19 February 1614: 'In consideration of our conjugal love etc, we grant to Queen Anne the capital messuage in East Greenwich called Greenwich House, with the Friers there, the gardens, orchards, etc, with Greenwich Park, and the houses and lodges within the park . . . to have and to hold for a 100 years should she so long live.' James's document is of great interest to Greenwich historians, listing as it does among Old Court possessions passed to the queen a number of the ancient outlying manors apparently long separated from Elstrudis's bequest, among them Brockley, Deptford, Lewisham, Lee, Lee Bankers, Shroffold, Eastcombe and Sayes Court. This is the old confusion between actual possession and manorial rights. Did the king's lawyers make a mistake, or was it after all not so easy to discard the legal bonds of a thousand years? Or is the explanation the simple one—that any British monarch might use what he took to be his royal prerogative at any time to override existing assignments of land?

The Earl of Northampton left Greenwich ill and unhappy, and died at his house in London four months later. But in fact his legal right to the Greenwich property must have been good, for though the king made a gesture of handing it back to the Cecils, it actually passed to Henry Howard's heir and nephew, Lord Thomas Howard, the Armada captain of the *Golden Lion,* immortalised by Tennyson—"Fore God I am no coward'—who was dear to James I as one of the discoverers of the Gunpowder Plot. Lord Thomas and his wife, now Earl and Countess of Suffolk, were given undisputed enjoyment of Greenwich Castle and members of the family lived in it for at least another twenty years, his daughter-in–law dying there in 1633.

The Earl of Leicester's mansion in its acre of walled garden behind the present pier, Northampton left to his great-nephew, Thomas Howard, Earl of Arundel. Although I have not been able to find that this was an old house, its position, coupled with the fact that after his father's attainder Robert Dudley would have little money to build anything new, suggests that it was. In 1522 some twenty-five Greenwich houses were considered luxurious enough to offer accommodation to the retinue of the visiting Emperor, Charles V, but the sites of very few of them can be pin-pointed with precision; somewhere near here must have been both the Norris house and that of the Carews.

Whatever its antecedents, the Leicester house had not been to Howard's liking; he had razed the place, with its forlorn, romantic memories, and built something which all his contemporaries conceded was magnificent. We do not know what the new house looked like, but it is possible to recreate something of its interior. Henry Howard had a taste for the exotic, and an inventory taken on 16 June 1614, the day after he died, accounts for his possessions not only in Northampton (later Northumberland) House, London, but in his houses at Greenwich.

His plate, consisting of long lists of standing cups and covers, livery pots, flagon pots, basins and ewers, pillar salts, trencher salts, candlesticks and tankards, fruit baskets, table baskets, platters, saucers, chafing dishes and spoons, all of gold, gilt or silver, came to more than £6,000. The 'howsolde stuffe' was luxurious and colourful, with tables and cupboards of 'walnuttree', tapestries from Flanders, 'Turkie' carpets and velvet-covered chairs and stools, their cushions embroidered with gold or silver thread and spangled with precious stones.

Greenwich Castle is described room by room; on the top floor there were a 'pallate chamber', a bedchamber, a closet and a gallery; an outer chamber, great chamber, withdrawing chamber and wardrobe occupied the middle storey; and a hall, domestic offices and servants' rooms were on the ground floor. Much of the furniture had probably been removed to London when Howard left, but in the main rooms there were still a number of rich leather hangings, in azure and gold, and crimson and gold, a chair and stools of crimson velvet with silk fringes, several Turkey carpets and a bed 'with a canopie of crimson damaske laced and frindged with gold'.

An even more magnificent bed was in the 'lower house' (presumably the ex-Earl of Leicester's). This was a 'blacke field bedstead painted with flowers and powdred with golde, with the Armes of my Lord of Northampton upon the head, 8 cuppes suteable [ie en suite].The tester and valance powdred with blew starres and spangles and slippes of several coulors and billeted, with 5 curtens suteable to the tester. A quilte of poppingey greene sarcenett lined with blew calicoe, stitched with black silk.' This bed, valued at £40, was sold to 'my lo. of Somersett', but other rich things in the house included a large Persian carpet and 'a paire of tables of Ebony inlaid with Ivorie and men suteable'—perhaps chess men.

Henry Howard was a rich man, gathering round him the precious objects of his day. But his great-nephew, Thomas Howard, Earl of Arundel, may be described as the first, and possibly the greatest, of our national collectors. John Evelyn named him as 'the father of Vertu in England, the great Maecenas of all politer arts and the boundless amasser of antiques'. He seems to have started collecting about 1615, soon after he inherited the Greenwich house, and British ambassadors all over Europe were asked to acquire for him 'pictures by Titian, drawings of Leonardo de Vinze, a book of Holbens, peeces of antiques in marble' and any other 'matters of arte' which might properly find a place in his gallery.

The man most actively concerned in the quest was Sir Dudley Carleton, our ambassador at The Hague. The procedure seems to have been that through his agents Carleton bought suitable specimens and had them shipped to London, where Lord Arundel could inspect them. On 9 April 1616 Edward Sherburn wrote to the ambassador: 'I have attended my L. of Arundell to Mr Fortry his house, where his L. with Mr Inego Jones, have fully reviewed the pictures.' In May, Sherburn was writing: 'I expect howerly to heare from his L. about the pictures. He told me the last week at Greenewich that he would send for them forthwith.' And by 11 July: 'This day my L. of Arundell gave direction to Mr Inego Jones in my hearing to pay me one day this week the £200: and to receive the pictures.' The money was to go to the partner-agents Daniel Nys and Nicholas Lanier.

On 3 January 1617 fell a great blow. George, Lord Carew, wrote to Sir Thomas Roe, ambassador at Constantinople: 'The Erle of Northampton's new-built house at Greenwich (by the negligence of servants) is burnt all but the gallerye to the ground, wherein the Erle of Arundell, whose house it was, lost a great part of his householde stuffe, which was of great value.' All London was horrified at the disaster, though Edward Sherburn was able to send a rather more cheerful note to Sir Dudley Carleton: 'On ye 2 January, ye Earle of Arundell's house at Greenwich was burned, and some rich moveables in it; though not to ye value as is commonly reported.'

Arundel seems not to have rebuilt his mansion; and an added loss locally was that the collection had now to be moved to Arundel House in the Strand, where a handsome new gallery had lately been built, looking on to the Thames. But he still retained the Greenwich site; a tax return of 1644 shows that by then there were twelve small habitations on it, all in his ownership. He was also to inherit from his uncle Suffolk the stewardship of the manor of Old Court.

For Henry Howard's third mansion, Lumley House, a different future had been planned. Here he was to establish his charity for twelve poor men of Greenwich and eight from his birthplace at Shottisham, Norfolk. Lumley House was pulled down and in its place was built Trinity Hospital—still there, a small seventeenth-century jewel in the Greenwich riverscape. Although restored in Victorian times, this little building with its central tower, quiet court and two acres of simple garden must look almost exactly as it did when it was first built.

The chapel was dedicated in the presence of a phalanx of Howards on 4 February 1617; in it there is a stained-glass window of great beauty, a sixteenth-century Flemish *Crucifixion*. Mr Brush, the present warden of Trinity Hospital, has told me the tradition that the window was once in another Howard house, and that it was rescued from a fire.

'This was the place,' he had written to King James in 1613, 'where he desired to lay his bones.' But in his anger and despair at losing, as he thought, the manor of Greenwich, Henry, Earl of Northampton, left instructions that he was to be buried at Dover Castle, of which he was Constable; and a handsome tomb by the king's master mason, Nicholas Stone, was erected in the chapel there. In 1696 this chapel fell into ruin; and his body and the memorial carved by Stone were transported back to his foundation at Greenwich where he now lies, this man whom his enemies described as a monster of wickedness, hypocrisy, obscenity—but who was thought of by his friends as the wisest of all the Howards.

At the river end of the Leicester-Arundel site was the Blew Boar, a building (not originally a tavern) named presumably in honour of Henry VII, whose blue boar, heraldically speaking, had triumphed over the white boar of Richard III. Early records of this fascinating house are unfortunately lost; possibly it became a secret rendezvous for Tudor support in Greenwich when it was still fashionable to be a Yorkist. By the end of the sixteenth century its ownership was the same as the mansion behind it, Robert Dudley selling it to Henry Howard in 1605. Somehow it passed in 1612 to Sir Nicholas Stoddard, a man whose acquisition of many Howard properties later resulted in a long series of law suits between the trustees of Trinity Hospital and his heirs. On 4 July 1616 Inigo Jones bought the lease of the Blew Boar and sold it next day to Thomas Howard, Earl of Arundel—a transaction which suggests he had been acting as Howard's agent. Later in the century it was to pass to William Smith, first of the Greenwich entrepreneurs, and to start a new life as the Ship Tavern, with the consumption of whitebait as a speciality of the house.

The chief Stoddard residence was Mottingham Place, built in 1560, and the family also owned lands in Lee. Sir Nicholas Stoddard seems to have been a man who fell out with his neighbours; early in the seventeenth century a complaint was made against him that he had cut down a quantity of the king's trees, converting more than sixty acres 'from good woodland to ill pasture'. There is a sad sequel to this accusation. So much of the abbot of Ghent's stewardship of his manors had been concerned with care of woodlands; and now, suddenly, comes the realisation that all are gone. Samuel Pepys, visiting the dockyard at Woolwich and finding that the *Royal James* was being constructed with iron knees, wrote to the chief shipwright, Sir Anthony Deane, to find out why and was told that, if nothing could be used but oak knees, 'then the King must build no more great ships. We have not one knee in the yard. All the King's forests and private men's timber within twenty miles of HM Dockyards on the Thames will not afford timber to build two first-rates in four years.'

John Chamberlain wrote to Sir Dudley Carleton on 21 June 1617: 'The Queen . . . is building somewhat at Greenwich which must be finished this summer; it is said to be some curious device of Inigo Jones, and will cost above 4000li.' What Inigo Jones was building, as all the world was soon to know, was a structure designed to straddle the Woolwich Road, so that its royal owner could pass from her flower garden to her park without spoiling her shoes. For, possibly since the days of Duke Humphrey who had formed it, this road had been known as the muddiest in all Europe; here was the spot—and not the northwest corner of the palace as described in *Kenilworth* by Sir Walter Scott—where Raleigh had put down his cloak for his sovereign. In a more permanent way, Inigo Jones was performing the same service.

The gatehouse overlooking the park had been a favourite point where people could congregate to view their sovereign; and it was part of the changed attitude of the Stuarts to the monarchy that the Queen's House, by arching over the road, should for the first time bring privacy and enclosure to the royal domains at

Greenwich—a privacy which was to be reinforced in 1619 by the replacement of Duke Humphrey's pale fence with a brick wall. The house, of course, was beautiful, a marvel; a superb architectural achievement, a hundred years ahead of its time. But its *raison d'être* was a non-starter. Coaches thundering through the narrow walled road, horsemen clattering over the cobbles, inquisitive onlookers, beggars, vagrants hanging about on the public highway under the central arch, all became an intolerable nuisance to the inhabitants. Almost as soon as it was finished (not for poor Anne of Denmark, who died when it was a half-completed shell, in 1619) plans were being made to divert the road, and a Via Regis was staked out to the northward in 1663; as usual, Greenwich imposed its own time scale and the present Romney Road, which resulted from the switch, was not brought into use until 1697.

The Queen's House is without doubt the most impressive monument of their reign that James and Anne left to Greenwich; but another aspect of the Stuart monarchy was to bring a more fundamental change. During the first quarter of the seventeenth century, service to the crown became *démodée*: or perhaps the opportunity to found a heritage no longer presented itself. Robert Cecil had raised on his service to the state the noble house of Salisbury; but the man who succeeded to most of his work inherited little of his great influence and none of his good fortune. Sir Thomas Lake took over Cecil's office in 1617; he was not able to sustain the position, and in less than two years he had fallen out with his daughter's in-laws (the Burghley Cecils) and was facing a somewhat contrived disgrace. A spell in the Tower and a fine of £10,000 put an end to his political career, and he retired to his house at Cannons, near Edgware. But part of the fortune he had hoped to amass was bound up with property at Greenwich.

The house on the Thames once owned by the Comptons had extensive gardens and orchards which had reached from the

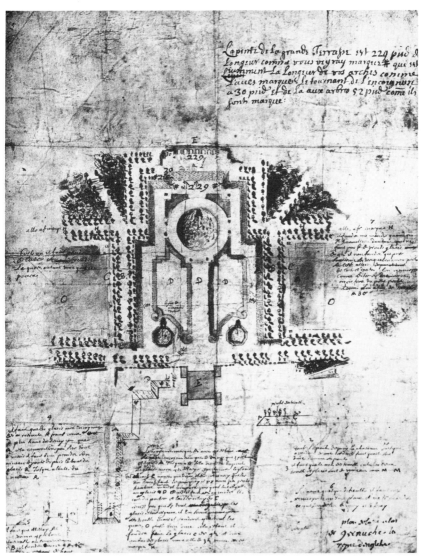

Map annotated by André Le Nôtre. An inscription in the lower right-hand corner reads: **Grenuche, la regne d'angleterre**

Etching of about 1700 by Francis Place, showing Crooms Hill from the park. The house built for Robert Osboldston in 1638, described by Pepys as "very pretty, and a fine turret at top", may be seen to the left, and in the detail below

waterfront to the park. Freed by their departure from the Greenwich court, this land now became available to the minor court officials who took over; and to begin with, much of it was acquired by the Lakes. Launcelot Lake, son of the royal secretary, was within the next twenty years to build houses on it for several members of the Lanier family, and to sell off a site to Henrietta-Maria's Clerk of the Kitchen, Sir William Boreman; and his son, Sir Launcelot, was to move to the old house in Crooms Hill, the Grange, and become the predecessor of another well-known Greenwich character, Sir William Hooker.

However we in our day may regard the Queen's House, it is apparent from their comments that contemporaries saw it with one unique difference. It was not originally thought of as a palace, not even as a residence; this was a piece of stage decor, a fancy embodying the new idea of permanent scenery for the masques. Possibly the building most impressive to the young Inigo Jones on his first visit to Italy had been Palladio's Teatro Olimpico at Vicenza; like the Whitehall Banqueting House which he put up for James in 1619, it was a permanent building where before the fashion had been for temporary ones. At Greenwich, Henry VIII's tilt-yard banqueting houses, however elaborate, had followed a progression from the merest ornamented tents of painted canvas and wooden poles. Anne's masques had been equally fleeting theatrical shows : but shows of a princely prodigality. To build the theatrical scenery in stone must have seemed the most royally prodigal act of all.

To quote the architectural cliché that the Queen's House was a hundred years ahead of its time is therefore in some ways a misrepresentation of its case. A hundred years was the time taken to convince other patrons, other rich men who wanted great and elegant houses for themselves, that it was respectable —indeed conventional and altogether right—to live in a piece of permanent classical theatrical scenery. That the Stuarts did this so early was due to a situation forced on them by the old palace's

decay and their own chronic lack of money: accepted so grace-
fully because of their common sense and their most uncommon
taste. After Anne of Denmark had died in 1619, the Queen's House
had been thatched over to protect the unfinished building from
the weather; but in 1629 Charles I gave it to his young French
wife, Henrietta-Maria, and at once a great new programme of
beautification was put in hand. Inigo Jones, the arch-masquer,
kept a sheaf of notes on the design, and wrote them into his copy
of Palladio. Nicholas Lanier and his cousins, scouring the continent for pictures and statuary to adorn the lovely toy, must
ever have had the new intellectual idea in mind—that this was to
be not so much a collector's gallery as the richest kind of theatrical decor. Among the painters invited to come and decorate the
walls and ceilings—walls with vistas of classical scenery, ceilings
with a dramatic peep into the heavenly firmament—were Gen-
tileschi, Rubens, Giulio Romano and Jordaens; Charles himself
must have regarded some of the painting as a sort of permanent
beauty chorus, since Jordaens received a special instruction from
the king to make 'ye faces of ye women as beautiful as may bee,
ye figures gracious and svelte'.

After their own earlier difficulties, after all the confused matri-
monial history of this place, Charles and his pretty young wife
brought it happiness at last; their house beautiful, their children
healthy, their garden (stocked with roses sent from France)
flourishing. John Philipott wrote of the queen's handiwork that
she had so 'finished and furnished her House of Delight that it
far surpasseth all other of that kind in England'.

Or was it after all too theatrical, too far removed from reality?
There was a space on one of the walls, left for a Rubens but
empty because his fee was too high. There was that thunder of
horses' hooves, boring endlessly into the heart of the house, taking away the peace of mind of its occupants. There was, too,
the dramatic pair of lasts, framing the twelve golden years of the

House of Delight. In 1629, when she first came to the house, Henrietta-Maria had been awaiting the birth of her first child. A long-distance control of this most important event was held by the expectant grandmother, Marie de Medicis, Queen-Mother of France; and the leading French midwife, Mme Peronne, had been ordered to hold herself in readiness. But ten weeks before the expected date of confinement, Henrietta at Greenwich did something too much for her frail physique (tired herself, it was said, by walking up the hill). No French expert could have made the journey in time; and it was the Greenwich midwife who was summoned in a frantic alarm—a panic which was added to when the woman, finding herself in the royal bedroom, with the august patient, fainted away and had to be replaced by a naval surgeon. The baby was born alive but died an hour after being christened Charles James. He was the last royal child to be born at Greenwich.

On 10 February 1642 Charles and Henrietta-Maria spent what was to be their final night together in the House of Delight —indeed, except for that heady, tented interlude at Oxford, his last home life of any kind. The queen was taking little Princess Mary to Holland for marriage with the Prince of Orange; the king was bound for the north, a long, troubled journey which would end seven years later on the scaffold.

The Queen's House, after Hollar (1637)

CHAPTER 10

Regicide and Restoration

It is difficult to assess the extent of the emotional and economic damage done to Greenwich by the Civil War. Although court activity must have put a good deal of spasmodic business into the hands of local traders, one cannot say its withdrawal would have brought them ruin. On the whole, the palace had been fairly self-supporting. Much of its food came from the king's own estates; Sayes Court, for instance, had kitchen gardens and orchards, herds of cattle, flocks of poultry on a large scale, all maintained for the express purpose of supplying Placentia. Many court officials would move about with the king, owing no more allegiance to Greenwich than to Whitehall or Richmond. On the other hand, service to the crown had been the mainstay of this place for as long as it had had a history; almost every citizen must have had some connection with the palace, if only expressed as family pride.

Yet, efforts to rouse the people met with no success. The Earl of Norwich brought a band of royalists into Greenwich Park in 1648 and camped there, hoping to recruit help for the king from among the king's ex-servants. But the response was virtually nil, and those men of Kent already joined had to disband and make their dispirited way across the river into Essex. Perhaps it was all too late—too long ago since Greenwich men had fought and died for a monarchial ideal, justice and the fair name of England. Too many dynasties had come and gone; possibly too many kings had shown too plainly, here, their failings. But some people at least found it unbearable to stay; John Reynolds, son of a very old-established Greenwich family, had his tax paid by a nominee in 1644 because of an unexplained absence. By the 1660s he re-appears as one of the founding fathers of Greenwich, Connecticut. Of the several towns named Greenwich in the eastern United States, most date from this period; and scattered freely over Massachusetts are the names of many other Greenwich families from seventeenth-century England.

We know most clearly the effect of the Commonwealth on the court musicians. These were the men who had moved into the mansions vacated by the nobility, or taken the more modest houses springing up in their orchards and gardens. In a way, they could be described as a new aristocracy of talent. Throughout the Tudor dynasty there had been a steady rise in the status of the music-maker, from troubadour to queen's favourite to Gentleman of the King's Chamber. It had been no accident that Mark Smeaton, the player on the virginals, had been among the line-up of men accused of adultery with Anne Boleyn. Mary, Queen of Scots' confidante, David Rizzio, was also a court musician, a guitarist. 'I know not,' wrote Nicholas Lanier to Sir Dudley Carleton in 1612, 'which is the more dangerous attempt, to turn courtier or clown.'

Nicholas Lanier (1588–1666) was the son of John Lanier, the sabeca player, and his wife Frances Galliardello, who lived in Crooms Hill. Himself a singer, Nicholas is credited with introducing into England the art known as *stylo recitativo*; he was also a composer and produced music for Ben Jonson's masques, *Lovers Made Men* and *The Vision of Delight*, both staged in 1617. Charles I, who made several of his kinsmen Gentlemen of the Bedchamber, created a new appointment for Nicholas Lanier, that of Master of the King's Musicke, with a salary of £200 a year. But an equally important side of Nicholas's duties was the seeking out of works of art for the royal collection.

Other court musicians who, like their parents before them,

made Greenwich their home included the string players Caesar Galliardello, Alfonso Ferrabosco, the Farrants and the Mells— 'the rare musitian called Mell', as John Evelyn wrote of David Mell. Of the ten Laniers in Charles I's orchestra, Innocent and Andrea were flautists, John and Clement played the sackbut, a younger Nicholas was a lutenist.

It was men like these who bore the brunt of the Greenwich disaster. All were thrown out of work; it is difficult to see how some of them lived. The Laniers in particular were owed large sums in wages. At the sale of the king's property arranged by the Commonwealth, creditors were allowed to accept goods in lieu of payment, and Nicholas and Jerome Lanier took home a number of the pictures they themselves had acquired for Charles I. Jerome's allocation was seven pictures at £201; Nicholas also took seven pictures, valued at £307. On a visit to the Grange in August 1652, John Evelyn noted in his diary: 'I went to see Jer. Lenniers rare Collection of pictures, especially those of Julio Romanos, which surely had been the Kings.'

Perhaps Jerome was too proud, or too loyal, to admit that his wages had not been paid. In any case, the pictures must have been handed back at the Restoration, for some careful research by Mr W. L. F. Nuttall, published in *Apollo* in 1965, has identified two of these Romanos—*A Sacrifice* and *Jupiter and Juno Taking Possession of Heaven*—both now at Hampton Court, together with one of Nicholas Lanier's acquisitions, Bellini's *The Concert*.

Other artists of the court were at the Greenwich sale; John Stone, son of old Nicholas, the master mason, bought the twelve Titian studies of emperors acquired by Nicholas Lanier from the Duke of Mantua. He and his brother Henry were both royalists and fought for the king, as did Alfonso Ferrabosco's son, Henry, whose later death in action left five children on the parish.

It was not only the pictures at Greenwich that the men of the Commonwealth prepared to disperse. A speculative builder,

John Parker of Hackney, was found willing to buy Greenwich Park and 'the materials of the Castle, Lodge, White House [ie the Queen's House], woods, 96 deer, stock of conies, rent of the priory, orchard, etc', for a total of £5,778 10s 1d. The palace by the river was divided up and sold off in lots. Colonel Robert Tichborne, one of those who had signed the king's death warrant, bought for £223 7s 6d the Hobby Stables, 'sundry barns and a parcel of ground adjoining', on the east of the tilt-yard; Richard Salmon acquired three houses to the east of this lot, a garden and the storehouse yard.

The old friary buildings, with the kitchen and privy gardens, went to Uriah Babington, who had been appointed Keeper of Greenwich House, garden and park by Charles I in 1634; he was also the royal barber and, according to Hasted, £3,814 in wages was due to him. The housekeeper's old house, charcoal house, woodyard office and woodyard were sold to Thomas Griffith. 'A messuage at the north end of the tilt-yard, the Queen's Garden' and part of the tilt-yard itself went to a Greenwich man, Henry Henn, for £224; the messuage named—'the mansion called Greenwich House'—seems actually to have been the Tudor palace itself. Henry Henn, like Babington, had been a servant of the court, being granted with his brother Hugh in 1639 the keepership of the queen's garden at Greenwich. It seems likely that both Henn and Babington bought their share of the royal possessions with the private intention of keeping them safe—an aim which soon became apparent and was frustrated.

Some of Cromwell's men may have had hesitations at the wholesale squandering of what was even then regarded as a national heritage; and whereas other royal properties had been put up for sale without qualm, there had been an initial reservation placed on 'the Honour and Manor of East Greenwich'. John Evelyn noted in his diary for 29 April 1652: 'We went this afternoon to see the Queen's House at Greenwich, now given by the rebels to Bulstrode Whitlock, one of their unhappy counsellors and keeper of pretended liberties.'

Whitelocke had found Greenwich not to his liking, and took over instead the Keepership of the Manor of Windsor. After the ensuing sale, but apparently before possession had been granted to all the buyers, it was decided that Greenwich House should be kept as a residence for the Protector, Oliver Cromwell himself, and the Parker sale at least was cancelled. All Commonwealth sales were to be annulled at the Restoration, and both Babington and Henn were compensated; Babington was installed in the housekeeper's house and Henn was given occupation of a small house near the tilt-yard which later passed to another court musician, Peter Guy, the flute-player, whose own house in Crooms Hill had had a charge put on it in 1650 by the ill-named Praise God Barebone.

But in the meantime the palace and grounds were subjected to an indignity that must have had its origins in envy if not hatred. Babington seems to have barricaded himself in the palace; he was forced out by one William Gunn, who proceeded to fill the royal apartments with 'disorderly persons'. Later, in spite of the ample provision of stabling, the state rooms of the Tudor palace were used to stable the Cromwellian soldiers' horses. Many things were ripped from the house and sold, and its wharf and outbuildings were allowed to fall into disrepair. Some effort was made to recover this last situation; timber from the tilt-yard was taken to mend the wharf, and James I's cockpit was dismantled and its materials used to restore the great barn. In 1653 the 'disorderly persons' were ejected from the palace rooms, which were then taken over as quarters for prisoners captured in the war with the Dutch.

While these indignities were being piled on Placentia, a minor version of the same tragedy was being enacted at the site of the old Compton house to the east of the palace. Here Sir Andrew Cogan, a London merchant and shipowner, had started to build himself a house, even for Greenwich of almost unprecedented grandeur. It was arranged round a central court-yard paved with Spanish tiles, and its walls were faced with elaborately carved consoles. Internally, the walls were hung with tapestries, the floors paved in black and white marble, and the oak staircase was massively ornamented with carving.

Cogan was an ardent royalist; already in 1642 he had amassed a collection of plate to send to Charles's funds in Holland (but it was intercepted and sequestered by Parliament). I think there is little doubt that this grand house—£1,107 was spent on glaz-ing, painting, carving and plasterwork alone—was built by a man who was a monarchist of an intense, old-fashioned kind, as some sort of compliment and support to the crown. Sir Andrew Cogan had been one of the very few who had joined the Earl of Nor-wich's royalist march on Greenwich in 1648; after the king's execution he fled abroad and received a number of commands signed by Charles II, among them an instruction to raise a regi-ment of 1,000 foot 'in Kent or elsewhere', and an appointment to the rank of admiral.

The Cogans returned to England with Charles II in 1660, having expended £40,000 on the Stuart cause. They should have had a great reward. But Lady Cogan died on 26 June, not four weeks after the Restoration, and Sir Andrew joined her in the grave the following October. By a piece of simple justice of which the king was surely not unaware, in the same October Gregory Clement, the regicide MP who had bought Cogan's £5,000 house in 1649 for £832, and furnished it with fire-places and other decorative features purloined from Placentia, was executed at Charing Cross.

The thoughtful years of the Commonwealth were to have a particular effect on Greenwich, in which the role of this place as the conscience of England was to enter a new phase. It may have been the impact of Puritanism; or the personal introspection that is often an accompaniment of national tragedy; or simple remorse at not having done more to save the king. But during the middle stretch of the seventeenth century there was to be a great upsurge of charitable activity here, hard to equal anywhere in England. Henry Howard's Trinity Hospital, amply endowed and ably run, was the obvious exemplar of this beneficence, but it was not the first. On 1 January 1544 the manor of Westcombe had passed from the Ballard family to John Lambarde, draper and alderman of London; and in 1574 his son William Lambarde, the historian, 'thanking God that He hath one step further by me amended our estate, and advanced our house', founded the Greenwich alms-houses known as Queen Elizabeth's College. It was the first foundation of the kind since the Reformation, a modest local charity rather than a rich aristocratic one, with among the Greenwich benefactors Edmund Chapman, who provided the land, William Dry, William Stanton, Captain Peter Watton, Edward Walrond, Joseph Macey, and Thomas Tallis's widow, Joan. It is still there, in London Road, opposite Greenwich railway station.

The fifties and sixties brought a flood of benefactions to the town, of which probably the most important was John Roan's 'to bring up so many poore town-borne children of East Greenwich at School, that is to reading, writing and cyphering'. There had been schools in Greenwich before, but they were for children of court servants and collapsed with the crown. John Roan had been a pupil of one of them; born about 1600, the son of a Sergeant of the Scullery to James I, he himself became Yeoman of His Majesty's Harriers, and continued to serve Charles I after the start of the Civil War until, falling into the hands of the Parliamentarians in 1642, he was stripped of all his possessions and died of his privations two years later. But he had already set in motion machinery for the endowment of his Grey Coat School; and his plans were put into execution by the charitable men and women of Greenwich. The school was opened in 1677 and like its source of income, the Roan Foundation, secured on many Greenwich properties, has continued ever since.

Another man who had an ambition to start a school was Sir William Boreman; his foundation, the Green Coat School, for the sons of seafaring men, was opened in 1672. Yet another, the Blue Coat School, this time for girls, teaching them to 'read, sew, spin, knit and do all sorts of household business', was started in 1700, its first treasurer being Mrs Flamsteed, wife of the Astronomer-Royal.

William Hatcliffe set up a charity for the provision of alms-houses; so did the vicar, the Rev Thomas Plume. It was a habit that was to continue into the nineteenth century, when two extensive charities were instituted—Penn's Almshouses and Jubilee Almshouses, for the comfort and help of the senior citizens of the town.

Other people left more modest bequests. Dame Dulcibella Boreman gave instructions that at her death her 'closet' should be sold and the proceeds devoted to building houses for four poor widows. Mrs Alice Clements left £100 'to be put out for clothing six poor widows, on the 7th of June her birthday, while Greenwich endures'. John Wardell bequeathed a rent charge of £6 10s for a weekly distribution of bread among fifteen poor widows; and Abraham Colfe, vicar of Lewisham, who made large charitable bequests to that place, also arranged for a weekly dole of bread to the Greenwich poor. William McGill added to Mrs Clements' charity in 1775, so that twenty-three poor widows might each receive on the founder's birthday a gown, shift, stockings and shoes. Nicholas Wigzell in 1720, dying in the house now numbered 34 Crooms Hill, left his wife 'the use of' his silver teapot, but also arranged a rent charge of £4 on property of his in Turpin Lane, 'for the benefit of the poor of Greenwich for ever'. The list of benefactions is a very long one; in his *Charities of Greenwich*, published in 1816, John Kimbell filled 292 pages, and even so does not exhaust them.

In 1661 Charles II visited his derelict palace of Greenwich, two gates in the park having to be broken open to let him in.

Inigo Jones had died of a broken heart in 1652, but the Queen's House drawings had been carefully preserved by his kinsman and pupil, John Webb, and plans were at once put in hand for a restoration. For Placentia the situation was different. The sordid condition of the Tudor building made rehabilitation there not feasible, and the great complex which is now the Royal Naval College was begun in 1662 with the setting out of the north-west pavilion, now known as the Charles II block.

The Restoration must have been greeted with a tremendous upsurge of joy in Greenwich. Ten years of proletarian rule had shown, in this place at any rate, spite and greed, reducing in the end to nothing but ruinous, squalid waste. It was hardly surprising that the inhabitants now looked forward with keen anticipation to a revival of its royal glories; and certainly Charles II gave every indication of wanting a grand new river palace here. His mother came back in 1662, reoccupying her House of Delight with a sad but exquisite elegance—twenty-four gentlemen in black velvet suits embroidered with gold attending all her public appearances; a dozen uniformed bargemen rowing her on the Thames, up and down between Greenwich and her London residence, Denmark House.

There were plans for a grand replanting of the park, of which the map (page 165) is one of the most interesting relics. Henrietta-Maria had spent much of her widowhood at the court of her nephew, Louis XIV, and had been present at the fabulous party thrown by Pierre Fouquet, Louis's finance minister, at his new house, Vaux-le-Vicomte. Here could be seen in all its grandeur the first large-scale work of the new young landscapist, André Le Nôtre. We know that Charles II wrote to his cousin Louis to ask if Le Nôtre might come to England to supervise the Greenwich layout. There is no evidence to show that he ever came; neither Pepys nor Evelyn, both interested in the park at this time, mention Le Nôtre in their diaries.

In 1955 the Comte de Ganay, Le Nôtre's biographer, dis-

covered in Paris a plan for Greenwich Park, or at least the part
of it in front of the Queen's House, laid out as a formal garden
with certain features very similar to the formal garden at Vaux-
le-Vicomte. It is annotated in two hands, one indisputably Le
Nôtre's, and in the lower right hand corner is an inscription:
'*Grenuche. la regne d'angleterre*'. Did Henrietta-Maria, dream-
ing in France of her House of Delight, forget to stress to Le
Nôtre the steep rise of Greenwich Hill?

Her son Charles, fascinated by the fountains and canals that
were such a beauty at Vaux, was still writing to his sister Hen-
riette on 17 October 1664: 'Pray lett Le Nostre goe on with the
modell, and only tell him this addition that I can bring water to
the top of the hill, so that he may add much to the beauty of the
descente by a cascade of watter.' But Fouquet's party had ended,
for him, in disgrace and ruin, Louis leaving abruptly for Paris
with a face like a thundercloud and a plan in his mind for the
immediate investigation of the French state accounts. Did it
gradually break in on the grandiose dreams of mother and son at
Greenwich that an imitation of Vaux-le-Vicomte would be an
inexcusable breach of etiquette?

Mr David Green, to whose kindness I am indebted for the
photograph of Le Nôtre's Greenwich plan, has made the sug-
gestion that André Mollet, another French gardener employed
by Charles II, and member of a family who taught Le Nôtre
much of his trade, might have taken over the layout while the
grander scheme was being reluctantly reconsidered. Certainly
Sir William Boreman, who was responsible for the actual work,
some time between 1663 and 1672 ordered the filling in of a
'basin' 16½ft square, at a cost of 4s 4d. And when he came to
make the twelve great grass steps up the face of the hill which
substituted for Charles' cascade, there was another excavation,
'part of the great pit', which also had to be filled. Meanwhile,
the work on the new palace proceeded expensively—between
1660 and 1665 more than £75,000 was spent—but slowly.

Samuel Pepys, moving his office to Greenwich on 24 August 1665 to escape the plague, found that the rooms arranged for him at the King's House were not ready. Again, visiting Greenwich in March 1669, Pepys 'landed at the King's House, which goes on slow but is very pretty'. Henrietta-Maria had left her House of Delight for the last time in 1665; on 10 September 1669, little regarded by the English, she died in France. Though Charles, on the water for other reasons, occasionally disembarked to visit his new palace, by 1675 it must have become apparent to the most ardent royalist that a great modern Placentia in the image of the old one—or indeed in any other image—was outside the scope of this king's pocket.

The absence of their royal overlord relaxed ancient inhibitions in certain inhabitants of the manor of Greenwich. The sites on the Compton lands had by now all been filled, as had the gaps in Crooms Hill. There now started a scramble for building land, and the ground outside the park—the 'waste' as it was called, between the wall put up by James I in 1619 and the king's private boundary which was the road—began to commend itself to speculators not too concerned about a legal title. The first to cast eyes on this spare land was Sir William Boreman, Clerk to the Green Cloth, the planter of the park; and to do him justice he did obtain crown permission in consideration of his philanthropic intention to found a school.

Boreman's piece of the waste was at the top of Crooms Hill, to the north of the park entrance there. Southward of it was a wide, flat stretch eminently suitable for building, which caught the attention of the king's farrier, Andrew Snape. Snapes had been royal farriers for about three hundred years; but with Andrew, a rogue judging by his face, described by Evelyn as 'a man full of projects', the loyalty to the crown this might have engendered seems to have emulsified into contempt. Snape enclosed the strip and built three villas against the park wall— an impertinence that would have been inconceivable in 1640.

He did not get away with it altogether: in 1675 the Manor Court threatened to level the houses unless some compensation was paid; and in the end crown leases had to be negotiated for all three properties. But there was plainly enough profit in the transaction for others to wish to emulate it. Sir William Boreman deciding to build his school down at the bottom, in London Road, his waste land was promptly acquired by Sir William Hooker. Soon afterwards, and in somewhat mysterious circumstances, three houses appeared on it. The illegality of all these houses, like those of Snape, was never really in doubt, and some of the long series of law suits brought by the crown to clear the title to the land are set out in Kimbell's *Charities of Greenwich*. The Boremans seem to have made a genuine attempt to put matters right by imposing on themselves the charitable burden of providing forty bushels of coal a year for the town's poor—a cheap penance of which Sir William Hooker was quick to avail himself, although he must have known that the land belonged not to the parish but to the crown.

Sir William Hooker—'a plain ordinary silly man I think he is,' wrote Pepys, 'but rich'—was a city merchant, a member of the Grocers' Company, sheriff of London during the years of plague and fire, and in 1673 its lord mayor. He had bought the Grange from Sir Launcelot Lake in 1665. It was he who, in 1672, built the beautiful little summerhouse at the end of the garden, one of whose functions, as a gazebo, was to look into the king's park over the twelve-foot wall. (Its architect was almost certainly Robert Hooke, partner of Sir Christopher Wren and one of the surveyors of the city of London after the Great Fire.)

An eighteenth-century schedule among the Grange deeds, dating from just after the Hookers' time, reflects much of the state which must have been enjoyed there by the Lord Mayor. There were three coach houses and stabling for eight horses; arbours, fruit groves and a walnut tree court besides the summerhouse. Within the house there was much wainscotting, many tapestries, and a series of marble fireplaces including one particularly elaborate one in red and white. Aldermen of the city of London were enjoined to keep up a certain state; during Sir William's tenure of that dignity—twenty-five years—at least one of them was dismissed for 'inability to live and maintayne himself in better sort and fashion'.

Sir William Hooker came to Greenwich to escape the plague. So did Samuel Pepys, and the diarist has given us a marvellous gossip's-eye view of local society during the autumn and winter of 1665. We know these men and women through their legal documents—leases, tax returns and wills. Pepys describes them as they were; it is all the difference between still photographs and the movies. He lodged with a Mrs Clerke on the east side of the palace. 'For three rooms and a dining-room, and for linen, and bread and beer and butter at nights and mornings, I am to give her £5 10s per month,' he wrote, and added characteristically, 'I am to pay dear.'

Through the pages of the diary we can walk with him about the streets of Greenwich, join him in a visit to 'the great music house the King's Head' near Billingsgate, run by the Laniers, or share in an evening spent with Captain Cock, Lord Brouncker and his mistress, Sir J. Minnes, Sir W. Doyly and Mr Evelyn, whereby the latter's reciting of some verses 'did make us all die almost with laughing'. We can visit with him that 'sober discreet man' Sir Theophilus Biddulph, who had bought Westcombe from the Lambardes in 1652, and was one of the crown witnesses at the trial of the regicides. We can go with him, Sunday after Sunday, to the parish church, old St Alfege's, where 'a company of fine people and a very good sermon'. On 3 December 1665: 'There I sat, near Mr Laneare, with whom I spoke, and my fat brown beauty of our parish, the rich merchant's lady'—Sir William Hooker's daughter, Anne, now married to Sir John Lethieullier.

We can eavesdrop on the many grave consultations he had

a ▲

b ▲

Greenwich chroniclers: a. John Evelyn. b. Samuel Pepys

Greenwich speculators: c. Andrew Snape. d. Sir William Hooker

c ▼

d ▼

*Sketches of old Greenwich by William Clarkson Stanfield, used by Captain Marryat to illustrate his novel, **Poor Jack** (1840).*
Elizabethan tavern in Church Street and, below, Fisher's Alley

with the vestry about the plague, and can hear, almost at first hand as it seems, the plea in September, 'very passionate methought', for a child smuggled out of an infected house in London and brought naked and illegally to Greenwich. 'Greenwich begins apace to be sickly,' he wrote to Lady Carteret on 4 September, 'but we are, by the command of the King, taking all the care we can to prevent its growth.'

Relatively speaking, Greenwich escaped the plague. In the black autumn of 1665 some 416 people died here, plus a further 374 in Deptford; curiously, the first six months of 1666 show a rise—to 423 in Greenwich and 522 in Deptford. Figures grim enough, but hardly to be compared with the 1665 autumn total of 3,466 for St Saviour's, Southwark, or the weekly London total of seven or eight thousand. Nevertheless, the statistics must have covered many a local tragedy.

East of the town, at the foot of the old manor of Combe, was Combe Farm, an isolated place on the Woolwich road where it is joined by what is now Westcombe Hill. Late on the day of 21 August 1665, Samuel Pepys at Greenwich wrote in his diary:

> Messengers went to get a boat for me, to carry me to Woolwich, but all to no purpose; so I was forced to walk it in the dark, at ten o'clock at night, with Sir J. Minnes's George with me, being mightily troubled for fear of the dogs at Coome Farm, and more for fear of rogues by the way, and yet more because of the plague which is there, which is very strange, it being a single house all alone from the town. But it seems they used to admit beggars, for their own safety, to lie in their barns, and they brought it to them.

Pepys spent the night at Woolwich with his wife; and on the next day, 22 August, wrote: 'I went away, and walked to Greenwich, in my way seeing a coffin with a dead body therein, dead of the plague, lying in an open close belonging to Coome Farm, which was carried out last night; and the parish have not appointed anybody to bury it, but only set a watch there all day and night, that nobody should go thither or come thence; this disease making us more cruel to one another than we are to dogs.' By 4 September he was recording the sequel: 'Walked home, my Lord Brouncker giving me a very neat cane to walk with; but it troubled me to pass by Coome Farm, where about twenty-one people have died of the plague.'

Combe Farm. A 19th-century photograph

CHAPTER 11

Speculation as an Art

To its seventeenth-century enterpreneurs, in spite of their occasional illegal annexation of land, Greenwich owes an incalculable debt. Never again were the great men of the nation to be under a duty to come to this place because of their attendance on the sovereign; but had not a handful of speculators built villas handsome enough to attract people of wit, elegance and sophistication—influential people whose advocacy of Greenwich was to give it a lasting *éclat*—little of the Greenwich environs could have been preserved; and the impetus to turn the royal estate into a great charitable foundation of a princely aesthetic kind might itself have been lacking. Much was owed, of course, to the beauty of the site; but more, I think, to an astonishingly visionary patronage of architects, which itself had roots of a surprising depth.

Queen Anne's masques, so often accredited to her as her own invention, arose directly out of the spectacles that had become a feature of the Tudor court. The people who put them on were, quite a large proportion of them, in the straight line of those Greenwich royal servants who had mounted the first one of all, at the Placentia Christmas of 1511. The musicians—Farrants, Ferraboscos, Galliardellos and Laniers—all had a pedigree extending through several reigns. Although names of men who built for Henry VIII at Placentia are known, including those who decorated the pretty conceits that were erected at banqueting times (Holbein painted a ceiling for one of them in 1527), it is not sure who designed them; nor can we be certain who wrote the entertainments. But without doubt the theatrical tradition was an unbroken one; Queen Anne's chief masque writer, Ben Jonson, and her chief designer, Inigo Jones, both born in 1573, spent their first thirty years of life as Elizabethans.

The masques were a species of private patronage of the arts, exclusive to the great nobles and the crown. It was the essentially personal links they forged with artists and promoters of the arts that were to lead to the great international culture of the seventeenth century. Thomas, Earl of Arundel's art collecting was an offshoot: not quite the same thing, but employing the same men. Inigo Jones was one of his closest advisers. Sir Dudley Carleton's network of English and continental collecting agents included a number of Greenwich men, among them Nicholas Lanier; but there was an important ancillary side to his efforts. The carriage of these fragile treasures back to England was a business both skilled and profitable, involving trader-packers, warehousemen and ship-owners. And the merchants chosen by Sir Dudley to undertake it may broadly be identified with the entrepreneurs of Greenwich.

Thus, the 'Mr Fortry' to whose house the Earl of Arundel's acquisitions were delivered in 1616 for transportation to his Greenwich gallery was almost certainly the Anglo-Flemish merchant John Fortrey (or de la Forterie) whose daughter Jane was to become the mother-in-law of Sir William Hooker's eldest daughter, Anne. The John Lethieullier Jane married was an Anglo-Flemish shipowner from Brabant, a member of the East India Company, with business houses in Cologne and Amsterdam as well as London; it was in his family's hulls that much of the delicate cargo was shipped. Robert Osboldston, a kinsman of the Lethieulliers, for whom was built the house on Crooms Hill so much admired by Pepys—'a very pretty house and a fine turret at top, with winding stairs, and the finest prospect I know about all Greenwich, save the top of the hill'—was a member of the

London Bridge Company, and likely to have been concerned in the all-important berthing and unloading of these precious cargoes. Sir Thomas Lake, as royal secretary, was the man responsible for payments to the merchant-carriers when they moved up from transporting Arundel's acquisitions to those of Charles, Prince of Wales.

The three-cornered liaison between merchants, artist-advisers and princely patrons came at a psychologically vital moment for Greenwich, bound up with the withdrawal of the nobility from the court here. Up till now, only the crown or the aristocracy had commissioned architects to work for them, and the idea that merchants should do this—and, moreover, do it speculatively— must have seemed extraordinarily daring and modern. The work of Inigo Jones and his fellow masquers at Greenwich provided, for men many of whom had themselves been involved in a minor capacity, an object lesson by means of which they could emulate their betters. For this was a social innovation as well as an artistic one.

Perhaps through a failure of nerve, the merchants did not patronise the leading architects; but the lesser men they commissioned were to form the nucleus of that very able second team who rebuilt so much of London after the Great Fire. Little documentation has survived; the houses are too small. Most attributions have to be made stylistically. But there is evidence of the great interest these Greenwich buildings aroused. One of the first, though in this case built for himself, was Sir Andrew Cogan's, whose impact on the regicides has already been described. In design it was almost identical with a house which caused tremendous excitement when it went up in Bishopsgate, erected by the ambassador to Turkey, Sir Paul Pindar; Sir Paul was another great benefactor of the Stuarts, lending them, it was said, more than £100,000.

On the evidence of the many seventeenth-century paintings of Greenwich, one might be justified in picking out the houses

put up by Launcelot Lake, both east and west of Placentia, as
the four-square, red brick edifices with dormer windows prominent in such pictures; and we might guess his architect to be his
cousin, Richard Ryder, a man known to have designed the
Apothecaries' Hall, London, in 1670, and himself a building
speculator. A survivor of these, a house once occupied by the
Laniers and likely to have been built for them by Lake when he
took over the Grange for his own occupation about 1656, is the
building now nos 16 and 18 Crooms Hill, also identifiable from
old views.

Architecturally speaking, the most mysterious house put up in
Greenwich during the first half of the seventeenth century was
that known as the Presbytery, Crooms Hill, just below the Roman
Catholic church to which it now belongs. It was built apparently
as a speculation by William Smith, hereditary Sergeant-at-Arms
to the King (founder of the Ship tavern), on land once owned by
the Swanne House. The Dutch gables and pilasters of brick
which are a feature of it were first noted in England in 1631
at the building of the charming small mansion known as the
'Dutch House', later to become Kew Palace. Historians of design
have long been puzzled about the architect of Kew; but at least
until the end of the eighteenth century there was an unquestioned
tradition that he was Dutch. The style is borrowed very closely
from the work in Amsterdam of Hendrick de Keyser, which
paved the way for the brilliant English manipulation of brick
that characterised the last quarter of the seventeenth century.

The house at Kew was built by Samuel Fortrey; and in the
same year, 1631, his cousin Peter Fortrey acquired the Eastcombe
part of the old Greenwich manor of Combe. This was also the
year when Nicholas Stone, who was working at Greenwich inter-
mittently for the whole of his life, invited his brothers-in-law,
Hendrick and Willem de Keyser, both architects, to visit him
and practise from his London studio. Dr Robert Mason, who
bought the Crooms Hill house from Smith about the same time,

was secretary to the Duke of Buckingham—that other great collector who in 1625 was appointed Ambassador Extraordinary to The Hague, and who the following year bought from Sir Peter Paul Rubens the collection of antique statuary sold to the painter by Sir Dudley Carleton in 1618. Buckingham, assassinated in 1628, left £500 to his secretary, and we may guess that this was the price of the Crooms Hill house.

Dr Mason was enormously proud of his little Dutch 'Hermitage', seeing it no doubt as an architectural achievement and innovation. In 1637 he invited Sir Edward Nicholas, Secretary of State, to come and view it. Sir Edward must have been favourably impressed, for he later acquired another example of these 'Dutch' houses, that at West Horsley, Surrey. Swakeleys, Middlesex, another of them, was built by Sir Edmund Wright, Lord Mayor of London in 1640, whose daughter Mary had married a member of the Smith family of Greenwich. In fact, all the 'Dutch' houses of the time may be linked with the Greenwich speculators. Not everyone approved of the new architecture; John Evelyn, invited over from Deptford to inspect it, noted in his diary for 25 September 1652: 'The house is a wretched one', though he admired Dr Mason's view.

Other buildings surviving from this fascinating hundred years of speculation and development include the handsome terrace at the foot of Crooms Hill on its west side, built in 1723 to house captains of the Seamen's Hospital—a private enterprise, apparently, since it does not figure in the Hospital terrier—and the beautiful building now called the Manor House, at the top of Crooms Hill on the west. This house was built for the London merchant Sir Robert Robinson in 1695, on crown land which had been licensed by James I in 1605 for the erection of farm buildings. The style is reminiscent of several city halls built after the Great Fire; the altogether exceptional wood carving on both front and back porches, and much of the interior ornament, echo closely the work of Edward Pearce, the Deptford carver turned architect who became Master of the Painter-Stainers' Company in 1693; a fellow Painter-Stainer was Robert Robinson, cousin of Sir Robert, and well known as a mural painter; another member, and Master in 1720, was Sir James Thornhill, who lived on the other side of Crooms Hill, in the house now known as Park Hall.

The efforts of the local entrepreneurs were, of course, soon to be hopelessly overshadowed by the greatest building project of them all, the highest aesthetic achievement, the noblest philanthropy; but the men engaged in the vast enterprise by the river did not confine their talents to it. Sir Christopher Wren had already crowned Greenwich Hill with the elegant little Observatory. Edward Strong, contractor for the Seamen's Hospital stonework, is now generally credited with the design as well as the building of Morden College, Blackheath. John James, joint Clerk of Works with Nicholas Hawksmoor from 1714, partnered him too in the new St Alfege's church in 1718, James doing the spire. He was really a carpenter, famous among his colleagues for beautiful joinery; and in his house, Hillside, most northerly of Hooker's waste villas, there is still some exquisite woodwork, although the house (now owned by the local authority) has been shamefully neglected.

Isaac Ware, Clerk of Works at Greenwich in 1736, was the man chosen by Philip, Earl of Chesterfield, to embellish the middle one of Snape's waste villas, which he occupied from 1748 until his death in 1773. Sir John Soane, an unsuccessful applicant for the job of Surveyor of the King's Works, compensated himself by building a whole new front wing for the Snape villa now called Macartney House; and Joseph Kay, Architect-in-Charge in 1825, in addition to his work on the Greenwich Hospital School, did a monumental replanning of the heart of old Greenwich town. And successive generations of unnamed craftsmen must have been responsible for much of the very fine unattributed detail in Greenwich houses throughout the long period—more than a hundred years—that the Hospital took to complete.

To William and Mary, the couple who inherited after the downfall of James II, the royal manor of Greenwich came to them as a wretched collection of fragments. Placentia squatted on its lovely site, no more than a heartrending muddle. Tilt-yard towers of the Tudor palace still stood up like indestructible molars in a mouthful of decay; the Queen's House, somehow now out of place and out of scale, sat uneasily at the foot of a tree-lined park which was quaintly unsuited to its landscape. Above what had once been the friars' church loomed Charles II's grand and beautiful block to designs by Inigo Jones, unused—indeed, unfinished—and now obviously unwanted. At the top of the hill, rising more than metaphorically, since it was built of the very materials, on the site of old Greenwich Castle, stood the new Royal Observatory, that brilliantly philanthropic gesture of uncle Charles II which, while it was to change immeasurably for the better the lives of his seamen, was also to make impossible ever again any private enjoyment of the park.

Who first suggested that Placentia should be transformed into a hospital for sailors is not now clear; but it is easy to understand how the idea, once there, could not be exorcised. The first letters patent were dated 25 October 1694; but Queen Mary died suddenly of smallpox two months later, and it was not until 30 June 1696 that John Evelyn, who had been appointed treasurer, was able to write in his diary: 'I went with a select Committee of the Commissioners for Greenwich Hospital, and with Sir Christopher Wren, where with him I laid the first stone of the intended foundation, precisely at 5 o'clock in the evening, after we had din'd together. Mr Flamstead, the K's astronomical Professor, observing the punctual time by instruments.'

By June 1705 Evelyn was able to write: 'The buildings now going on are very magnificent.' It was a word directly applied to her plans by the foundress; Nicholas Hawksmoor had frequently to defend the Hospital against the charge of over-lavishness by reminding critics that Queen Mary had 'enjoined Sir Christopher

Wren to build the Fabrick with great Magnificence and Order'.

Sir James Thornhill, who started his decorative scheme for the Painted Hall in 1707, and worked on it for nineteen years, cherished a private ambition to succeed Sir John Vanbrugh in his office as Architect-in-Charge at Greenwich Hospital. He acquired land at the south-east corner of the park, apparently with the intention of building there a mansion designed to show off the architectural skill which should gain him the job. But this was the very area chosen by Vanbrugh for his own estate, and Thornhill wisely retreated to the opposite side of the park, where tradition assigns to him the middle one of Hooker's waste villas (Park Hall). Search for documentaion on this point has so far failed to produce anything more concrete than the letter by James Wolfe, the conqueror of Quebec, written from the Snape villa now called Macartney House, in which he speaks of 'our neighbours, the Thornhills'.

Sir John Vanbrugh's contribution to the Greenwich scene was suitably dramatic and well sited. On a hill to the east of the park, between the ancient promontory which had once been crowned by Greenwich Castle, and the equally prehistoric earthwork once the stronghold of the Trinovantes at Charlton, he built his own fortress. Vanbrugh's Castle, at the top of Maze Hill, was for a long time known locally as Bastille House, under a mistaken notion that it was a replica of the prison—in which Vanbrugh had actually once been incarcerated. But it is likely to have taken the form it did because that was all he could afford.

It is a poor man's castle, small, poky, brick instead of stone, narrow and sharp rather than solidly foursquare—a fortalice in shorthand. Was it designed as a happy theatrical tribute to the reputation of the place; as a bit of personal pomposity; or as the intuitive response to a sensed antiquity by a not inconsiderable artist? And how much was Vanbrugh swayed by his own heredity —this man whose mother was a great-niece of Sir Dudley Carleton, and whose grandfather was a citizen of Ghent? (That

Ghent had never relinquished a moral claim to the manor of Greenwich we know from a letter of 8 February 1705, in which the Superior of St Peter's complains to the Bishop of Tournai about the 300-year-old annexation of their possessions here by the heretics.)

In 1699 the manor of Old Court 'with its demesnes and the lands called Queen's lands' was sold to Sir John Morden, of Wricklemarsh, Charlton, for £1,276 10s, and by his will of 1708 vested in trustees for the benefit of Morden College, Blackheath. It was another great charitable foundation for the district; Sir John Morden was a merchant trading with Turkey and the Levant, and his endowment was made for the relief of Turkey merchants who had fallen on evil times. Sir William Boreman had been granted a 99-year lease of Old Court in 1676, but this was bought out by Morden from his widow for £9,000. The projected sale of crown rights made it necessary at last to sort out exactly what was the manor of Greenwich and where lay the manorial properties. The task, a herculean one, was entrusted to Samuel Travers, Surveyor-General to the Crown, and his mandate was to examine the holdings of 'His Majesty's Lordship or Manor of East Greenwich, in the county of Kent, with all its Rights, Members and Appurtenances, Palace, Park and Demesne there, parcel of the Ancient Possession of the Crown of England'.

In *Charities of Greenwich,* John Kimbell publishes the findings; they run to fifty-five closely printed pages, and the facts embedded in them are of priceless value to historians of Greenwich. But one sad paragraph tells almost all that need be said on the mysteries attaching to the ancient possessions of Old Court.

To the Seventh Article: That, upon a strict enquiry, the jurors cannot find there are any ancient deeds, evidences, court rolls, or books of survey, relating to the said lordship or manor of Greenwich, now remaining; but it appears by the oath of Mr Elwood, who was clerk to Mr Tooke, the late steward, that about eleven years since, he carried some court rolls of this manor to Sir William Boreman, since deceased, at his house in London, and believes he took a receipt for the same, but cannot now find it; but affirms that Mr Yardley, then Clerk of the Kitchen to the Queen Dowager, was present when he delivered the same rolls to Sir Wm Boreman.

So much for the lost history of Greenwich: but at least we know who lost it.

Outside the palace, things were not well with the town. In spite of the large sums collected by John Evelyn, many of them subscribed by citizens of Greenwich (one of the greatest benefactors of all was Robert Osboldston, son of the builder of the Crooms Hill house), the erection of the hospital benefited hardly at all the ordinary inhabitants. Poor, loyal Greenwich, abandoned by the crown, worn out in its service, was near to facing disaster. All those charitable bequests to widows serve to underline one thing—the extreme hazards faced by seamen in the days of sail.

In November 1703 occurred perhaps the worst storm the British Isles have ever had to endure. This was the tempest that destroyed woods and forests all over England, caused large-scale flooding, damaged or demolished uncountable buildings, blew down the Eddystone lighthouse, and sunk an unknown but very great number of large and small ships. The Thames estuary seems to have got the full force of the gale; in London more than £1 million worth of damage was done; Evelyn at Deptford reported that 'house, trees, garden &c at Sayes Court suffer'd very much.'

It was the terrible toll in lives of men at sea that most affected Greenwich; of the sixteen naval vessels sunk, *Northumberland* and *Restoration*, both Deptford built and locally manned, were lost on the Goodwin Sands with all hands; another Deptford third-rate, *Stirling Castle*, lost 379 out of her complement of 446. The Woolwich fourth-rate, *Mary*, was overwhelmed with a loss of 343 men; the boom-ship *Mortar* lost all its complement of sixty-five. Many smaller Thames-based craft not in the navy (and therefore not in the record) were likely to have been sunk while fishing or trading.

To the town thus stricken in 1703, 1707 brought an additional disaster. On 22 October of that year Sir Cloudesley Shovell, leading his squadron back from the Mediterranean, became entangled among the outlying rocks of the Scilly Isles and lost in a few moments his flagship, *Association*, and *Eagle* and *Romney*, the last-named a Woolwich ship with a number of Greenwich men in her complement. Not two weeks earlier, the Woolwich-built *Devonshire* had been blown up in action and many local sailors lost.

It must have seemed to bereaved families of the town that God was wholly against them; for at 4 am on the bleak morning of 29 November 1710, without any warning the roof of their parish church fell in, shattering the monuments and damaging the walls beyond repair. In the unhappy conditions then prevailing, the sum of £6,000 which was estimated to be the cost of a new church was quite unraisable. 'The sudden fall,' wrote Greenwich's nineteenth-century historian, H. S. Richardson, 'was occasioned by a hidden defect in the largest pillar, that fell, bringing the roof with it. (Supposed by reason of excavations for interments.)'

Historically, as well as spiritually, it was a tragic loss; the old church possessed memorials to Edward the Confessor (who had confirmed the charter to Ghent); Duke Humphrey of Gloucester and his wife; Henry IV's 'dear squire' John Norbury; family memorials to the Lambardes, Hatcliffes, Hookers, Boremans, Lethieulliers, Masons, Robinsons—and indeed almost every Greenwich citizen of mark since 1100.

A Case of the Inhabitants of Greenwich was put before Parliament in February 1711; it set out the local situation with dignity and restraint :

The inhabitants had lately expended several hundred pounds

on their church, which they believed might have stood for centuries. The town had for twenty years been depopulated of its wealthier inhabitants, and the larger houses had been empty for years. The wealthiest persons being tenants at will, were movable and had no local interests. Nine-tenths of the inhabitants were seamen, watermen and fishermen, and the tradesmen were in low condition, through giving long credit. So many heads of families had been lost in the great storm, Sir Cloudesley Shovell's misfortune and accidents of war, that upwards of 3,000 widows and children had become chargeable to the parish.

As a result of this petition, the Act for building fifty new churches in London and its suburbs was expressly broadened to include Greenwich. The present St Alfege's was the result, the beautiful church designed by Nicholas Hawksmoor, with carving by Grinling Gibbons—John Evelyn's protégé, 'that incomparable young man Gibbon, whom I had lately met with in an obscure place by meere accident as I was walking neere a poor solitary thatched house, in a field in our parish, neere Says Court'.

Among those buried in St Alfege's is James Wolfe; he wrote to a friend in 1751 that his father, then living near the church, talked of buying for £3,000 'the prettiest situated house in England', and he later described the view from the garden, through the front gate, as the fairest prospect. The house was the first of Snape's villas; the view, that rejoiced in by both Pepys and Evelyn—still there today, with Paul's dome and Westminster spires only a little dwarfed by the high-rise flats, the Vickers building and the Post Office tower.

Wolfe stayed a lot in his parents' house at the top of Crooms Hill, in the intervals of his military service. The Lawson family at one time held a lease of the house to the north (the last of Sir William Hooker's waste villas, now called the White House), divided from the Wolfes' property only by the Crooms Hill entrance into the park; so it was probably here that he met

Elizabeth Lawson, the girl he was to love and court unsuccess-
fully for four unhappy years. Elizabeth Lawson died unmarried
in 1759. Wolfe's father died in that year too, only a few months
before the triumph and death at Quebec. While all England
rejoiced at the victory, only in the hero's home town were
festivities forbidden, out of consideration for the twice-bereaved
wife and mother at the top of Crooms Hill.

The middle one of Snape's villas passed, an unwanted legacy
from his brother in 1748, to Philip Stanhope, Earl of Chesterfield.
It was to grow upon his affections until six years later he was
echoing the words of Dr Robert Mason and calling it 'my
hermitage. This, I find, is my proper place.' In 1751 he wrote
to the Bishop of Waterford: 'The *furor hortensis* has seized me,
and my acre of ground here affords me more pleasure than
kingdoms do to kings.' 'Could you send me,' he wrote to Solomon
Dayrolles on 23 December 1748, 'some seeds of the right
Cantelupe melons? It is for Blackheath that I want it.' The
cultivation must have been successful, for a few months later he
was writing: 'I shall keep a little room for you at Blackheath,
where I will refresh you with the best ananas and melons in
England.'

'Blackheath,' wrote Chesterfield to Dayrolles on 19 June 1750,
'is now in great beauty. The shell of my gallery is finished [he,
too, aspired to be a great collector], which, by three bow-windows,
gives me three different, and the finest, prospects in the world.'
(The house now belongs to the Greater London Council, and
members of the public may enjoy the still ravishing views from
the three bow-windows.)

Lord Chesterfield's later years were saddened by the death of
his son, so loved, so fretted over, and by his own bad health.
It is a pity that his deafness cut him off from his neighbours at
Greenwich, since we might have learned much about them from
his letters. His quickness of tongue survived a decade of illness,
though not everybody found him witty. Dr Johnson, who disliked

him, complained that it was not wit but puns; Horace Walpole commented acidly that no man deserved more to be witty since no man tried so hard. But at least one joke set all Greenwich laughing; when a mutual friend asked after Lord Tyrawley, who had taken a lease on Vanbrugh's Castle from the widowed Lady Vanbrugh, Lord Chesterfield could murmur in reply: 'Tyrawley and I have been dead these two years but we do not choose to have it known.'

The saddest little villa of them all was Snape's last, built on the waste at the south-west corner of the park. Montague House took its name from George Brudenell, who had married Anne, granddaughter of John Churchill, Duke of Marlborough, and through her acquired the dukedom of Montague. Perhaps the house was recommended by Sir James Thornhill, who did a number of commissions for Ralph, 2nd Duke of Montague, including the rather infra dig painting of his coach. The house passed to George Brudenell's daughter, Elizabeth, Duchess of Buccleuch, who leased it in 1801 to Princess Caroline, estranged wife of the Prince Regent. Here came Sir Thomas Lawrence in the same year to paint her portrait and that of the Princess Charlotte. Here, too, came malicious gossip. Lawrence was an attractive man, and no doubt the princess, deprived of a normal married life, enjoyed his sympathy.

The *Dictionary of National Biography* gives Lady Douglas as the caller who reported seeing a young male child in Montague House. In the inquiry of 1806 known as the Delicate Investigation, Lawrence put in an affidavit expressing his incredulous innocence of the implied charge. The princess's own defence, sent to the king on 2 October, said: 'Mr Lawrence mentioned his wish to be permitted to remain some few nights in the house, that, by early rising, he might begin painting on the picture before the Princess Charlotte or myself came to sit. . . . While I was sitting to him at my own house, I have no doubt I must often have sat to him alone, as the necessity for the precaution of having an attendant, as a witness to protect my honour from suspicion, certainly never occurred to me.' The picture itself, painted far too flatteringly—the gay, talented young mother, the vivacious, adoring child—was given away to Lady Townshend, the princess's Mistress of the Robes; but Queen Victoria bought it back in 1843, and it is now at Buckingham Palace.

Irritated beyond reason by his incompatible wife, the Prince Regent had Montague House pulled down in 1815. If his idea was to exorcise the memory of their kind and friendly neighbour from the people of Greenwich, it did not succeed. One of the most often repeated reasons for his rejection of the princess was the statement that she did not wash. Yet a constantly recurring activity at the houses she was to occupy during her long, wandering exile was the erection of an outside bath-house with a sunken bath. Such a one at the Villa Vittoria, Pesaro, where she went in 1818, was decorated with blue and white tiles and reached by a small, steep stairway. Its description comes remarkably close to the odd little structure, now in Greenwich Park but once within the grounds of Montague House, overlooked by 'Prinny' when he removed the traces of his wife's occupation there.

Vanbrugh's Castle, drawn by William Stukeley in 1721

CHAPTER 12

The Developers — and After

On 23 December 1805, the body of Admiral Lord Nelson ended at Greenwich its long voyage from Trafalgar, and was laid on a black-draped dais in the Painted Hall. The coffin was covered with a pall of sable velvet and flanked with his coronet and sword. (Later, the blood-stained uniform, cut away for the surgeon's pitying gaze, was to be put on exhibition in the same place; it may still be seen in the National Maritime Museum.) Three days were given to public homage; on the first, according to *The Times*: 'Before eight in the morning every avenue from the metropolis was crowded with vehicles of every description. . . . When the gate was thrown open, above ten thousand persons pressed forward for admittance.' At closing time a huge disappointed throng had to be turned away.

During these three days of public homage it was estimated that over a hundred thousand souls had made the pilgrimage to see their dead hero. The occasion was a serious one, and did everybody credit; but the realisation that such a colossal press of people could pour at will into the confines of Greenwich was to bring with it a long shadow. John Evelyn, visiting the first Blackheath Fair in 1683 and noting in his diary: 'It was pretended for the sale of cattle, but I think in truth to enrich the new tavern at the bowling green, erected by Snape', had even then added the comment: 'I suppose it too neere London to be of any great use to the country.'

In 1800 the population of Greenwich was some 14,000, a

figure which could be swelled by the 2,500 inmates of the Seamen's Hospital. (The population of London at this time was about 850,000.) The vast majority of Greenwich inhabitants were Kent born and bred, men and women whose forebears had watched, and of course helped to form, the town's long history. But the weave had important alien threads in it.

The revocation in 1685 of the Edict of Nantes had driven many thousands of French Huguenots to seek refuge in England from religious persecution. Perhaps because it was here that Protestantism had been born, or perhaps because of its history as a place of conscience, they chose Greenwich as their sanctuary. Their leader was the Marquis de Ruvigny, and to the apartments placed at his disposal in the Queen's House came many English who wished to honour men willing to give up everything for their faith—among them John Evelyn, who had struck up a warm friendship with de Ruvigny, 'now my neighbour at Greenwich . . . a person of great learning and experience'. To Ruvigny, too, hurried escaped Frenchmen anxious to trace family or friends separated in the agonising flight.

A number of these French refugees settled permanently in Greenwich, and their names stud its subsequent records. On 6 October 1687 John Evelyn stood godfather at St Alfege's to the first-born son of his Huguenot friend, Sir John Chardin, 'a very curious and knowing man'. Sir Daniel Layard, Physician to the Princess of Wales, had a house on Crooms Hill which, judging from old prints, looks remarkably like another of the Lethieullier-Fortrey Dutch houses. Daniel Josias Olivier (among whose descendants is Lord Olivier, the actor) bought from Mark Cottle's successors the house on Crooms Hill first lived in by Robert Osboldston. Near the church lived the Teulons, whose descendant, Samuel Teulon, was to become a prominent Victorian architect. Farther west, in Church Fields, was a house— it was to be rented in 1745 by the parents of James Wolfe— occupied by John Ducarel and his wife, Jane. John is described in Huguenot records as a clerk; a picture belonging to his son, Dr Ducarel, formed the subject of the famous engraving of the Palace of Placentia, done by James Basire for the Society of Antiquaries in 1767 (page 68).

The Huguenots were quickly accepted into the life at Greenwich. John Ducarel's sister married one of the Lethieulliers; Julia Chardin, sister of John Evelyn's little godson, became the wife of Christopher Musgrave, grandson of Sir Andrew Cogan, the royalist. Sir Daniel Layard's eldest son married Elizabeth Ward of Lee, whose family had a long history of royal service at Placentia. And no doubt many other instances of intermarriage could be found in the parish registers.

But although the French influx must have brought pleasure and intellectual enrichment to the town, physically it produced little change, though Peter de la Motte, one of Ruvigny's lieutenants, was given a licence to enclose land at the top of Crooms Hill on its western side which had previously been in the occupation of George Shott, the king's matchmaker. The 99-year lease was dated 1722, and a condition in it that he 'lay out the sum of £300 in the building of a new Brick House on the said ground and pay a fine of Five guineas to the use of the poor' foreshadows the erection of Crooms Hill House, later the childhood home of General Gordon's mother, Elizabeth Enderby. About 1806 this land passed into the possession of the Randall family, and Kimbell records that in 1815 there were three houses on it. The site is now occupied by Beaver Trust flats.

One of the last mansions to be erected in Greenwich was that put up at the north-east corner of the park, at the foot of Maze Hill, on an 8-acre stretch of what had hitherto been crown meadowland. The site was bought in 1699 by a London brewer named Gregory Page from the Old Court estate of Sir John Morden; and here rose a handsome house of red brick with stone dressings, the grounds being laid out in formal lawns and terraces. Sir Gregory obtained permission to replace the park wall in front of his house with iron gates and railings—a precedent which was to be followed by the residents of Crooms Hill in 1842.

At Sir Gregory Page's death in 1720, his fortune invested in the South Sea Company passed in trust to his son, also Sir Gregory. Of the three trustees, one was for selling, one for hanging on; the third gave a lucky casting vote, and at a time when other investors faced huge losses in the bursting of the South Sea Bubble, young Sir Gregory found himself the richer by £200,000. He used the money to buy Sir John Morden's Wricklemarsh estate at Blackheath, where he pulled down the old house and built himself a new one, to the designs of the local architect, John James.

There must have been an inherent desire for change in the Page family. The great new house at Wricklemarsh, 'one of the finest seats in England belonging to a private gentleman', and built at a cost of £90,000—'never a better built house in the world,' said one of the workmen employed to demolish it, 'one whose walls would have stood for several hundred years'—was sold by his heir at Sir Gregory's death in 1783 to John Cator of Beckenham for no more than £22,550, and taken down about four years later for the laying out of the estate in speculative villas, among them the houses in what is now Blackheath Park, and the terrace called The Paragon—which tradition tells us incorporates the colonnades from Wricklemarsh.

From the very earliest times, Greenwich had both dominated and been dominated by its position at the heart of a network of river crossings. The important ferry over the Thames here, from the wharf at Billingsgate to the one at Horseferry House on the Isle of Dogs, was the main link in a chain which began with the crossing of the Ravensbourne at Deptford Creek. Over on the Essex bank this same chain continued with a crossing of the river Lea at Blackwall, and the river Roding where at its mouth it was called Barking Creek. The Lea has already been indicated as the quickest route from Greenwich to the Cattuvellaunian stronghold at Wheathampstead. Perhaps more significant, the Roding would be the speediest way for the men of Trinovantum to reach their Trinovantian territories in Essex.

Near the Ilford wharf on the Barking Creek was an ancient way called Werepath, which seems to have been the start of a customs-free land route to Greenwich's London possession of Weremansacre (or Waremansacre). The track followed the edge of the marsh westward, crossing the Lea just north of the East India Docks, and ending up at the London Billingsgate. One may draw the obvious conclusion that this was an alternative route for Trinovantian traffic with London when the river was barred by enemies or bad weather; but over and above that assumption is the fact that the Barking, Ilford and Wanstead manors which bordered the Roding as it approached its mouth had a long and detailed history curiously contiguous with that of Old Court.

For an undetermined period of its life, Ilford wharf, like the London Billingsgate, belonged to Greenwich. At certain times it was used exclusively for cross-Thames trade, and Queen Elizabeth reserved it for the dispatch of Essex-collected produce to her palace of Placentia; this, too, was the way the stones were shipped by Henry VIII from the despoiled Barking Abbey for his renovations at Placentia in 1540 and 1541—a piece of archaeological evidence that was uncovered by the antiquary Smart Lethieullier, when he excavated the abbey ruins in 1724. (That same Smart, grandson to Dame Anne, née Hooker, was responsible for the handsome memorial to the Lethieullier family, still to be seen in the churchyard at St Alfege's.)

For the purpose of this history, the relevant part of the Essex–Greenwich connection may begin with a young woman named Jane Trappe, described in Drake's *Hundred of Blackheath* as the daughter of a Tournai merchant, but almost certainly a member of the Trappe family of Lewisham. Her first husband, John Le Thieullier, merchant of Cologne, died in 1593; after a brief second marriage Jane brought her two Lethieullier children to England in 1604, taking them to the Ilford manor of Aldersbrook, the Essex home of the Osboldstons, who were her kinsmen. By 1693 her grandson, Sir John Lethieullier, had acquired from the Osboldston co-heiresses all except one of the Ilford and Barking estates previously held by that family.

One of these estates was Malmayns, once owned by Robert Dudley, Earl of Leicester, and closely linked with the Dudley possessions in Greenwich. (This manor in the 1670s was in the hands of a man named Young, whose widow was to cross the water and become the second wife of Sir William Boreman.) Another was at Dagenham, where in 1707 an appalling breach occurred in the river bank, flooding a thousand acres of Essex marsh and causing the formation of a sandbank in the Thames which threatened to stop all shipping.

Breach House, the handsome office building from which the work of repairing the river bank was directed—an engineering operation which cost more than £40,000 and took thirteen years to accomplish—was to become a centre of entertainment for the gentry and the home of whitebait dinners. It was the pulling down of this house by Sir Charles Hulse, whose mother, Mary Lethieullier, had inherited it from her uncle Smart, that resulted in the transfer of the whitebait dinners to Greenwich. The Hulses already lived south of the river, Richard Hulse having taken over the unexpired portion of the Earl of Chesterfield's lease at his death in 1773.

In 1680, Sir John Lethieullier built for himself and his wife, Anne Hooker, a mansion near the Brockley road in Lewisham, on land which seems to have been inherited from the Trappes. And although the family retained their links with Essex, no doubt crossing backwards and forwards by the ferry as Pepys had done—'July 15, 1665: Mr Carteret and I to the ferry-place at Greenwich, and there stayed an hour crossing the water to and again to get our coach and horses over; and by and by set out, and so towards Dagenhams'—Lewisham House became the family headquarters until in 1776 John Green Lethieullier sold it to a Mr Sclater of Rotherhithe.

It was another Rotherhithe man, John Dagge, mariner of that town, who bought the last Osboldston manor at Ilford—Downshall—from John Hyde, grandson of Elizabeth Osboldston, the last co-heiress. With the money obtained, John Hyde bought from Christopher Mason, grandson of Dr Robert Mason, Buckingham's secretary, the old Swanne House lands behind the Mason house on Crooms Hill, which were later to be developed as Hyde Vale. It is an ironical twist in the eastward expansion of London that, as this part of Greenwich was to be developed by an Essex man, Hyde's Essex manor of Downshall was to be acquired and sold for development by a Deptford market gardener named Edmonds.

What marked the end of an era in Greenwich was the Wricklemarsh débâcle, pointing as it did the way for a whole new race of entrepreneurs. No longer was it a case of the great houses of medieval noblemen being replaced by more manageable villas for the gentry; now those villas themselves, with all their carefully acquired architectural individuality, the gardens and grounds of a country-house expansiveness, were suddenly seen to be vulnerable to the more profitable business of putting up terraced town houses for the respectable middle class, with behind them the rows of neat, yellow-brick cottages for the poor.

In Crooms Hill in 1812 old Mrs Olivier died. She left the Osboldston house to her grandson, Daniel; but Daniel had his own house elsewhere, and the Greenwich property, with its barns and arbours, and the cherry orchard of five hundred trees, was sold to a speculative builder who knew all about Wricklemarsh, having not only watched the process of demolition there, but bought one of the Paragon houses for himself. This was Launcelot Loat, and, on a rather humbler scale, he now proceeded to do a Wricklemarsh in Greenwich.

The Osboldston house was demolished and George Street (later King George Street) was laid out for development, with its miniature side streets and its Presbyterian chapel. Launcelot Loat may also have been responsible for the Circus (now Gloucester Circus) houses nos 21 to 42, a development of about 1791 on land behind Crooms Hill once owned by the Hookers. Certainly the architect of these houses, Michael Searles, was known to him, since Searles was the designer of The Paragon.

Right at the end of the old Osboldston orchards was a patch of ground rented from Mrs Olivier for a market garden by a man named Royal. He bought it at her death and was presumably the builder of a small double speculation which rose on it, nos 65 to 87 Royal Hill and their counterparts in King George Street, nos 3 to 25. Either he or his father had already been responsible for the transformation of Gang Lane (its name a legacy from the Danish occupation of 1012) into a flourishing Georgian neighbourhood, ultimately achieving that acme of eighteenth-century respectability, some assembly rooms; here, these consisted of a lecture hall and reading room on the site of the present Borough Hall. The shift from the historic centre of Greenwich, round town well, parish church and dock, had perhaps been dictated by its sheer weight of years and the gradual impracticability of any more regeneration. Gang Lane changed its name to Royal Hill, and Greenwich old town began to cast about for a grand redevelopment.

The chance came in 1831, when a Greenwich Hospital Improvement Bill was put before Parliament to enable the Hospital Commissioners to acquire the tangled property to the west of the old royal palace. Joseph Kay, already architect for the Royal Hospital School (located in the Queen's House and what is now the National Maritime Museum) was the man responsible for the monumental replanning which produced Nelson Road, Clarence Street (College Approach), King William Walk and the new, more westerly Market, as well as the area round the pier.

There was a general clearance which inevitably lost to the town much of its medieval atmosphere. The Friars' Road had been closed in 1697 at the start of the Wren rebuilding of the palace; now the new road which had replaced it, running up from the river to the park through the grounds of old Copped Hall, was also done away with, as were Stableyard Street, Rood Lane (once the home of the Ferraboscos) and Tavern Row. Not all the old waterfront disappeared immediately; Fisher Alley (or Lane), the east-west street of ancient houses running from Garden Stairs at the river end of Church Street to the river stairs at the old Ship Dock, was still intact ten years later, and the census of 1841 shows that most of its inhabitants were still connected by trade with the water. In it there was, too, an Arundel eating house, close on the site of the old, burnt-out mansion of Thomas Howard.

Nelson Street became a centre of bankers and brokers. The trade in the new market was mixed, meat, fish and dairy produce being sold beside the vegetables, with a clutch of stalls for pots and pans, cheap glass, ribbons, braids and pedlars' haberdashery. Stockwell Street, from the habit of two thousand years, remained the very heart of the town; for here, at the dog-leg bend with Crooms Hill, was the town well, the drinking-water supply for both men and animals, which must have been sunk, or at any rate used, by the Trinovantes. Several old wells have been uncovered in Stockwell Street during the past twenty years, one of them by its masonry dating to the Romans. A subsidence on 5 March 1970, on a spot outside the doors of the Greenwich Theatre, where a few hours earlier had stood a car conveying Princess Alexandra to a performance there, revealed the casing of a large well, with a tunnel leading out of it in a north-easterly direction.

Into the short length of Stockwell Street was crowded a multiplicity of shops. In 1840 there were two butchers, a grocer, a poulterer, a fishmonger, a wine merchant, a goldsmith, a perfumier, a stationer, three drapers, two milliners, a hairdresser, two oilmen, two dressmakers, bootmaker, furrier, chemist, engineer, a haberdasher, a straw hat presser and a painter—though whether the last was concerned with pictures or house walls is not revealed in the records. Reading the old rate books, struck again and again by the numbers of stables, one can understand the contempt embodied in the colonial's phrase 'a one-horse town'. Greenwich in the early nineteenth century must have been a thousand-horse town or more.

The river, however, dominated. It was no accident that nine-tenths of the merchants who figure in the history of Greenwich were shipowners, that the East India Docks had been placed on the nearest piece of vacant land, that a majority of all the British explorations from the fifteenth century onwards were financed or victualled or manned from this small stretch of Thames. The river view up stream from Greenwich Reach to the Pool was a fabulous one. James Boswell, on 30 July 1763, described a day trip he made with Dr Johnson; they embarked from the London Billingsgate—the traditional setting–out point for Greenwich—and Boswell wrote: 'We were entertained with the immense number and variety of ships that were lying at anchor, and with the beautiful country on each side of the river.' Philip, Earl of Chesterfield, writing in his ponderous French to the Marquise de Monconseil a few years earlier, also described the scene: *'Babiole est située dans un des parcs du Roi, à cents pas de la Tamise, ou l'on voit tout les jours une cinquantaine de gros vaisseaux marchands, et quelques vaisseaux de guerre, qui vent et qui viennent.'*

Greenwich people, almost to a household, would have a personal connection with these ships; it was to provide homes for the wives and children of the seamen and the men who served the fleets that speculators like Launcelot Loat, Robert Royal, Tyler with his 'New Town' off Trafalgar Road, and the managers of the Morden College and Roan School investment funds put up their rows of Regency houses that are still so characteristic of the Greenwich scene.

The skilled hands would be housed in small, trim cottage terraces like George Street, Pelton Street, Prior and Brand Streets; the slightly grander double-fronted houses in the side-streets would be for mates and shipwrights, and the all-important shipping clerks. Officers would come, many of them, from among younger sons of houses round the park, and almost without exception they would have received their education at Weston's Academy in King Street (now King William Walk). Thomas Weston, Assistant Astronomer-Royal to Flamsteed, was already in 1715 teaching reading, writing and navigation to 'ten sons of seamen who had lost their lives in the service of their country'—an activity which formed the foundation of the Royal Hospital School. Weston's Academy, under a succession of head-masters, lasted for more than two centuries; among its pupils were James Wolfe, Jack Jervis (afterwards Earl St Vincent) and the boys of the Mason family. Like many others, Christopher Mason became an admiral—indeed it has been said that by Nelson's day half the flag-officers in the fleet had received their instruction at the Greenwich Academy started by Weston.

In 1782 the school moved to a house at the foot of Crooms Hill, on the site once occupied by the mansion called Audley House; about six years later it was taken over by Fanny Burney's brother Charles, and run by himself and his son, Dr Charles Parr Burney, for nearly forty years until the whole establishment was moved to Portsmouth about 1825. The school grounds, which stretched as far as Royal Hill, became the last central Greenwich speculation, Burney Street being formed when the old house was pulled down in the 1830s. Some of its outbuildings remain, at the side of no 6 Crooms Hill. Another speculation almost contemporary with it resulted from the demolition of Sir Daniel Layard's house in 1835, with nos 38 and 40 Crooms Hill being erected on the site, and Crooms Hill Grove laid out in its garden.

One outer development which remained concerned the oldest estate of them all, apart from the king's. On the west side of Lime Kiln Lane (now Greenwich South Street) were some lands known as the Ditches. These had belonged to the old Swanne House of the Courtenays. Passing with other Swanne House land to the Masons, they were sold by Christopher Mason (father of the admiral) to Sir Ambrose Crowley in 1754. Crowley was a Newcastle ironmaster who amassed a fortune of £300,000 out of making anchors for the navy. Early in the eighteenth century he acquired Cogan House and renamed it after himself. Crowley House grew even more magnificent than its predecessor, and various legends began to be propagated that it was the authentic palace of the Tudors—a compliment of a sort, which would have delighted the royalist Sir Andrew. Sir Ambrose died without male heirs, and his granddaughter, Elizabeth Crowley, taking a dowry which included £200,000 and the Ditches to her husband, John, Earl of Ashburnham, the latter part of her portion was developed in the nineteenth century in the pleasing small streets west of Greenwich South Street whose names commemorate her husband's family.

Crowley House itself was eventually sold for little more than its site value, and pulled down some time after 1860, to rise again in a dramatic metamorphosis as the Greenwich Power Station of 1906—a huge, overbearing blot on the beauty of the Reach, whose function was to make the electricity that powered London's trams.

The one other centrally placed mansion was the house built by the older Gregory Page at the bottom of Maze Hill. This remained, in its eight acres of garden, until 1821, when the house was pulled down and the Regency terraces in Park Vista, Park Street and Trafalgar Grove were formed from its grounds —a charming little enclave which was to be broken into but not quite destroyed by the eastward extension of the railway in 1878. The Page mansion, vacated by young Sir Gregory when he bought Wricklemarsh in 1720, was taken over by a succession of Greenwich gentry, of whom much the most important were the Vansittarts. Henry Vansittart was a man of mixed European descent, who included among his forebears de Keysers, Fortreys and Lethieulliers. He bought the Page house in 1768, and settled his wife and children there while he continued a distinguished service with the HEIC in India. His wife, Emilia Morse, was the daughter of a Governor of Madras; and he himself was Governor of Bengal.

In the last days of 1769 the sailing ship *Aurora*, taking him back to his duties in Bengal, sank without trace; but his widow and her young family continued their association with Greenwich. Nicholas, the second son, grew up to have a distinguished career in politics, and served as Chancellor of the Exchequer from 1812 to 1823. He was created Lord Bexley, and Bexley Place, on the north side of London Road—for he, too, joined the ranks of Greenwich speculators—is named after him. There is a certain piquancy in recalling that by his purchase of Foots Cray Place he became lord of that manor of Ruxley once held by Malger the Fleming, and later by Gregory de Rokesley, the London merchant who performed such useful financial service to Edward I.

The Page house was not the most easterly in Greenwich; that position was held by the old, and once plague-ridden, farmhouse at the foot of Sheepgate Lane (now Westcombe Hill) which some antiquarians believe to have been the ancient capital messuage of the manor of Combe before it was split up by the Ballards into its three component parts. Combe Farm lands, taking something over a hundred men to work them, stretched all along the Woolwich road from Conduit Lane (later Vanbrugh Hill) in the west to Lombard (Lambarde) Wall in the east, covering about two hundred acres of marsh meadow, orchard and market garden. Greenwich Marsh itself, the great, north-stretching loop of land ending at Blackwall Point, was still largely an undrained cattle pasture, its only buildings the centrally placed watch tower, to guard against who knows what ancient enemy, and the gunpowder magazine and its wharf about a quarter of the way along the west shore.

In 1802 this old magazine was bought by Henry Vansittart's elder son, also Henry, and demolished to make way for a wharf belonging to the shipping firm of Samuel Enderby and Sons. Unhappily, the Enderby papers are not available to the Greenwich historian, and without them one cannot say precisely when this firm came to Greenwich. There was plainly a close link with the Vansittarts. A sister firm which worked in partnership with old Samuel Enderby was controlled by the Champion family of Lee, whose own local connections included Sir Samuel Fludyer of Lee Place, and Lord Dacre. The Enderby trade was whale oil, and it was Enderby vessels voyaging to pick up oil gleaned by the whalers of Nantucket that had their return cargo, East India Company tea, thrown overboard into Boston Harbour in December 1773.

The American War of Independence forced such men as Enderby and Champion to reconsider their trading patterns, and in 1789 the Enderby brothers fitted out a ship for a secret mission round Cape Horn. The vessel was the *Emilia*, called after Henry Vansittart's mother and without doubt having Greenwich men in her crew. Her voyage was the true start of the southern whaling industry; and when she returned to Greenwich in 1790 with a full cargo of sperm oil, Samuel Enderby wrote in a letter brimming with pride: 'The whales of the South Pacific are likely to be most profitable.'

Other Enderby or Champion ships soon followed in *Emilia*'s wake, among them *Britannia, Albemarle, Admiral Barrington, Speedy, Elizabeth and Mary, Salamander, Albion, Alexander* and *Greenwich*—all famous whalers in their day. The outward cargo was more often than not convicts, and the close working with the government that this meant, plus the ancillary carriage of supplies to the settlements, gave the Enderbys not only an important stake in the development of Australia and New Zealand, but a chance to explore the Antarctic.

As early as 1793 the Enderby whaler *Rattler*, under the command of an ex-Captain Cook man, Lieutenant Colnett, RN, was sent under Admiralty auspices to discover whale movements in the South Pacific. James Weddell in 1822, with two Enderby ships, the *Jane* and the *Beaufoy*—the latter no more than 65 tons —sailed farther south than any man before him; and John Biscoe in 1831 discovered a black, mountainous country rising out of the Antarctic ice and named it after his employers, Enderby Land. Thomas Melville of Boston had captained Enderby's *Britannia*, and in *Moby Dick* his grandson, Herman Melville, was to write a glowing tribute to the famous British whaling house. The pride he expressed must have found an echo in many a Greenwich sailor's home.

Samuel Enderby lived at the top of Crooms Hill, in Crooms Hill House, whose doorway survives in the flats on the Randall enclosure. His brother Charles lived on Greenwich Marsh, in a lonely house (it is still there) beside Enderby's Wharf. Other than three cottages beside it, and a small colony by the ancient landing stage on the east side of the marsh, called Ceylon Place and consisting of a row of cottages and the Pilot public house, built in 1801, there was nothing.

In this pair of twin landing places, giving as they did alternative anchorages for an easterly or westerly wind, must lie the key to the maritime development of Greenwich—and, for that matter, of London. At no other locality in the whole length of the Thames could such suitable natural facilities be found for vessels which depended for their motive power on the force of wind in sails. Even after the docks were built, for another couple of centuries these two anchorages had continued to provide a quick, private means of communication between owners and ships at the start or finish of a voyage.

To the large number of Honourable East India Company officials and men already named in this account could be added many, many others, among them Sir William Langhorne, of Charlton; Christopher Boone, of Lee; the Larkin family, who captained the ships and lived at the top of Crooms Hill; Mr Snodgrass, the HEIC's Chief Surveyor, who built himself a handsome house with a fabulous river view at the top of Blackheath Hill (still there, now no 89), and had his name borrowed and immortalised by Charles Dickens.

The coming of steam ended all that. Within a handful of years wharves had sprung up all round the Blackwall split, their choice of site being conditioned not so much by any geographical uniqueness as by the accident of finding open riverside land within handy reach of London. From now on the only premises concerned with sail would be those yards like James Piper's which built Thames sailing barges. The whaling industry drifted elsewhere, the Enderby family worn out by the expense of exploration whose benefits were more quickly exploited by their rivals. With the East India Company abolished in 1858, its great ships' riding lights would now swing only in the memories of old Greenwich longshoremen. The Enderby rope factory, with its rope walk near the Ship and Billet end of Blackwall Lane, had been burnt down in a spectacular fire in 1845, but who knows how much longer it would have remained viable?

The industrial development that now engulfed the marsh brought a need to build communications; their provision meant the importation of a new community into the still predominantly Kentish town—Irish construction workers whose names feature largely today in the electoral rolls of Marsh Ward. Homes for them and for the work force of factories that must be in reach of riverborne coal took priority over the food-bearing activities of Combe Farm, and the last agricultural land was given up for housing in 1905.

These changes were brought about by permanent newcomers; but temporary visitors were also making a mark. Although the Bowling Green Tavern (later the Green Man) and the Chocolate House Assembly Rooms at the top of Blackheath Hill continued to attract their own kind of reveller, once the park was opened to admit friends of the seamen patients at Greenwich Hospital, about 1705, it became a focal point for Londoners on holiday. Soon afterwards the fair, or the merry-making that accompanied it, moved there, and the sport known as 'tumbling' down Observatory Hill took hold of the Cockney mind.

There grew up vested interests of many different weights, all eager to turn Greenwich into a national pleasure ground. Pickpockets and vagabonds came; cheapjacks of many kinds set out their stalls; travelling theatres opened; Wombwell's Menagerie arrived; a dancing booth capable of holding a thousand couples was put up in Creek Road. Ships—steamships after 1838—brought human cargoes bent on making the most of their brief leisure, unloaded them at the pier and spewed them into the park. A Greenwich railway, raised above the teeming population of south London on a series of brick arches from London Bridge, was opened on Christmas Eve, 1838, terminating at a temporary station in London Road, while permission was awaited to carry the line farther east.

The broken heads, legs, even necks that resulted from the hill-rolling down what was left of Charles II's giant steps up Observatory Hill, together with the flourishing trade done by the footpads, and the bawdy and obscene nature of much of the entertainment, aroused the anger of the inhabitants of Greenwich. There was no historical tradition for the fair, and in any case these revellers had not come because of an intrinsic interest in this place. In 1780 the accidental rediscovery of the Blackheath Cavern had produced a volume of excited speculation as to its origins; but what had first been expeditions of genuine historic inquiry soon degenerated into entertainment as riotous and bawdy as that of the fair, and in 1854, after several occasions on which the candles had been fed with asafoetida and then put out, the cavern was closed.

From the 1820s Greenwich residents tried to rid themselves of the horde of destructive humanity that descended on them at fair time. A parish petition dated 24 April 1825, and signed by people like Mrs Enderby and Miss Vansittart, talks about 'yearly unguarded sufferance' and complains that 'the numbers of the profligate part of the lower orders have been increased' and that 'a very great addition is made to this evil by the open and powerful incentives to licentiousness.' The petition adds that scenes commonly witnessed at the fair 'are offending against the best feelings of Christian morality'.

It was the familiar Greenwich conscience speaking—successfully in the end, since the fair was finally suppressed in 1857. By then another menace, more evil in the long term, and more destructive than anything that Greenwich had faced since the attempted Commonwealth dispersal, was threatening its citizens. The men who ran the railway, obsessed by the enormous number of users, sought permission to run an eastward extension of the line, on a pseudo-classical viaduct across the level stretch of the park in front of the Queen's House.

Protection of the environment was a novel concept in Victorian England. However cynical it might have been, the plea of public interest put up by the promoters was a very troublesome one for nineteenth-century men and women to refute, and we do well to remember that the long and bitter struggle they sustained throughout the 1840s, 1850s and 1860s was for the heritage we now enjoy. When the battle dragged into a somewhat weary success in 1878, with the eastward extension of the railway forced into a vibration-proof tunnel underneath the town and park, age or death of many of the original combatants prevented any large-scale celebrations. But this was really the pinnacle of the Greenwich achievement, and all that follows is an epilogue.

For the climax of the days of sail coinciding with the completion of the building of the town had produced a situation almost classical in its attainment: nothing added, nothing wanted. The mixture of medieval, Georgian and Regency streets satisfied the needs of the inhabitants; the rise of industry was to keep them prosperous. No more villas were destroyed, no more speculation was undertaken; with the exception of the marsh (where indeed development still continues) and occasional infilling, there is no Victorian building in the centre of Greenwich. If we can forget the power station on the river bank, that added to it, the first years of the twentieth century saw an increase of grime as probably the most significant change in the place, other than the break-up of the Angerstein estate at Woodlands—last remnant of the old manor of Westcombe.

Violent alteration came with war, when bombs falling between 1939 and 1945 on London Road (now Greenwich High Street) and Stockwell Street caused gaps in the ancient trading pattern which, incomprehensibly, the local authority refused to allow to be filled. A planning blight was put on the heart of the town; indeed, the opportunity was taken to inflict on the old streets some wholesale, irreparable destruction. In two disastrous weeks in the 1960s, the descent of gangs of demolition men on Stockwell Street saw a thousand years of Greenwich's habit of life torn down and carted away as rubble. An equally insensitive attack on London Road in 1970 witnessed the same sorry mess.

Across the thus bared heart of this very ancient place it is now planned to run a motorway, for the convenience of commuters from the new council estate on the Woolwich marshes, called Thamesmead. The 4 acre site abutting on Stockwell Street and the parish church—scene of an urban growth which has progressed through 2,000 years—is now to be subjected to a 'council development', although at the start of 1972 it was admitted by Greenwich Borough Council that they had no money to do it in other than the cheapest possible way.

The plans formulated by the Greater London Council and the London Borough of Greenwich, not publicly admitted to but not denied, include a six- or eight-lane motorway through the park on the flat land in front of the Queen's House, going one better than the nineteenth-century railway promoters with its culmination in a nineteen–lane intersection beside St Alfege's church, on the very spot where Archbishop Alfege was murdered by the Danes in 1012. What words can be used about the present or future of Greenwich in the face of such silencing annihilation? Beyond this local authority vandalism, how clearly do the men who call themselves planners understand the portent in their latest decision: that by denying to London the old commercial use of the Thames, they not only ensure the decay of Trinovantum and its child-city upstream, but make inevitable the transfer of the capital of England to Southend?

★   ★   ★

Since 1973, when the above words were written, some planning changes have been made, some threats have receded. Others remain, and have intensified. We now know that town councils as a breed are adept at destruction but without creative skills. The need is for constant vigilance.

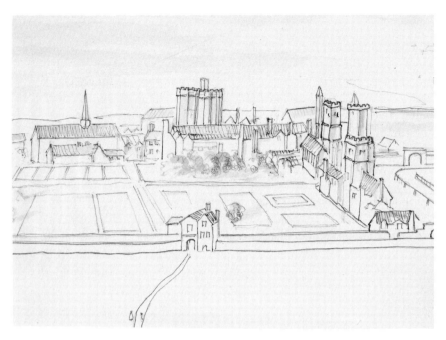

The Park Gatehouse, from Wynegaerde's drawing of 1558

Ruins of Duke Humphrey's Tower, about 1670

Sir Andrew Cogan's riverside house, later called Crowley House, and sometimes confused with Placentia. It stood on the east side of Trinity Hospital (below), founded by Henry, Earl of Northampton, in 1613

The Green Man Tavern, Blackheath Hill; a "project" of Andrew Snape

"Tumbling" in Greenwich Park

Montague House, home of the Princess of Wales from 1801

The house seen from Greenwich Park. It was pulled down in 1815

Stockwell Street in the 19th century. The house set back on the left is No 6, Crooms Hill

Old houses at the river end of Church Street

View from the Royal Observatory in 1804, looking towards London across a Thames full of shipping

Acknowledgements

We are grateful to the following for giving us permission to reproduce copyright illustrations: *Cover*, The National Maritime Museum, London. 1, Crown Copyright, Ministry of Defence; 6, Greenwich Public Library; 9, by kind permission of Viscount De L'Isle, VC, KG; 11, 12, 16 (a and b), National Portrait Gallery. Illustrations not acknowledged are from the author's collection.

Bibliography

AGNEW, Rev David C. A. *Protestant Exiles from France*. 2 vols, 1871

BEDDOE, John. *The Races of Britain*. 1885

CAMDEN SOCIETY. *An English Chronicle*. Davies (ed), 1856
Letters of Margaret of Anjou. Monro (ed) 1863
Rutland Papers. Jerdan (ed), 1842

CHAUCER, Geoffrey. *Life and Records*. M. Crow (ed), 1966

CHESTERFIELD, The Earl of. *Letters*. Lord Mahon (ed), 1892

CHETTLE, George H. *The Queen's House, Greenwich*. 1937

COLVIN, H. M. *Biographical Dictionary of English Architects*. 1954

CORBETT, Julian S. *Drake and the Tudor Navy*. 1899

CROFT-MURRAY, Edward. *Decorative Painting in England*. 1962

DAKIN, W. J. *Whalemen Adventurers*. 1934 (Australia)

DOUGLAS, Rev James. *Nenia Britannica*. 1793

DRAKE, H. H. (ed). *Hasted's Hundred of Blackheath*. 1886

DUVIVIER, C. *Recherches sur le Hainaut Ancien*. 1865 (Belgium)

ERLANGER, Philippe. *Marguerite d'Anjou et la Guerre des Deux Roses*. 1961 (France)

EVELYN, John. *Diary*

FORBES, Allan. *Towns of New England and Old England*. 1921 (USA)

GARMONDSWAY, G. N. (ed). *Anglo-Saxon Chronicle.* 1953

GEOFFREY OF MONMOUTH. *History of the Kings of Britain*

GILDAS. *De Excidio et Conquesta Britanniae*

GILES, J. A. *Six Old English Chronicles.* 1896

GREENWICH AND LEWISHAM ANTIQUARIAN SOCIETY. *Transactions*

GUEST, Lady Charlotte. *Mabinogion.* A. Nutt (ed), 1892

HADFIELD, A. M. *Time to Finish the Game.* 1964

HAKLUYT SOCIETY. *Narratives of Voyages Towards the North-West.* Rundall (ed), 1849

The Voyages of Robert Dudley. Warne (ed), 1900

HAMILTON, Olive and Nigel. *Royal Greenwich.* 1969

HARDEN, D. B. (ed). *Dark-Age Britain.* 1956

HARLEIAN SOCIETY. *The Visitation of London, 1633, 1634, 1635*

Pedigrees of the Knights. Le Neve (ed), 1873

HASTED, Edward. *History of Kent.* 12 vols

JULIUS CAESAR. *De Bello Gallico*

KENT ARCHAEOLOGICAL SOCIETY. *Archaeologia Cantiana.* See index for Greenwich references

KIMBELL, John. *Charities of Greenwich.* 1816

KIRBY, J. W. *History of the Roan School.* 1929

LAMBARDE, William. *Perambulation of Kent.* 1570

LANSDELL, Henry. *Princess Aelfrida's Charity.* 1911

LEGGE, Mary D. *Anglo-Norman Letters and Petitions.* 1941

L'ESTRANGE, Rev A. G. *The Palace and the Hospital.* 2 vols, 1886

LYSONS, Rev Daniel. *The Environs of London.* 1796

MARGARY, Ivan D. *Roman Roads in Britain.* 1967

MARRYAT, Captain. *Poor Jack.* 1840

MEANEY, Audrey. *Gazetteer of Early Anglo-Saxon Burial Sites.* 1964

NENNIUS. *Historia Britonum*

NICOLAS, N. H. *The Battle of Agincourt.* 1833
Privy Purse Accounts of Elizabeth of York
Wardrobe Accounts of Edward IV
Privy Purse Expenses of Henry VIII
PAGE, William. *London : its Origin and Early Development.*
1923
PEPYS, Samuel. *Diary*
RICHARDSON, H. S. *History of Greenwich.* 1834
RICHMOND, I. A. *Roman Britain.* 1963
RIPLEY, William Z. *The Races of Europe.* 1899
ROGER, P. *Noblesse et Chevalerie du Comté de Flandre,*
D'Artois et de Picardie. 1843. (France)
ROLLS SERIES. *Brut Y Tywysogion.* Williams ab Ithel (ed),
1860
Munimenta Academica. Anstey (ed), 1868
Political Poems and Songs. Wright (ed), 1861
Waurin's Chronicles of Great Britain. 1864
ROUND, J. H. *Geoffrey de Mandeville.* 1892
SEATON, Ethel. *Sir Richard Roos, Lancastrian Poet.* 1961
SITWELL, Edith. *Fanfare for Elizabeth.* 1946
SMITH, John. *A History of Charlton.* 1970
SOCIETY OF ANTIQUARIES. *Archaeologia.* See indexes for
Greenwich references
VAN LOKEREN, A. *Chartes et Documents de L'Abbaye de*
Saint Pierre au Mont Blandin a Gand. 1869 (Belgium)
VARENBERGH, Emile. *Histoire des Relations Diplomatiques*
entre le Comté de Flandre et L'Angleterre au Moyen Age.
1874 (Belgium)
VERCAUTEREN, Fernand. *Actes des Comtes de Flandre.*
1938 (Belgium)
VICKERS, K. H. *Humphrey, Duke of Gloucester.* 1907
VICTORIA COUNTY HISTORY. *Essex*
Kent
Surrey

WEBSTER, A. D. *Greenwich Park, its History and Associations.*
1902

WEBSTER, Graham and DUDLEY, D. R. *The Roman
Conquest of Britain.* 1965

WEEVER, John. *Ancient Funeral Monuments.* 1631

WEISS, R. *Humanism in England during the 15th Century.*
1941

WHISTLER, Laurence. *The Imagination of Vanbrugh and his
Fellow Artists.* 1954

WOOD, Margaret. *The English Medieval House.* 1965

WOOLWICH ANTIQUARIAN SOCIETY. *Transactions*

Index